CONTENTS

Notes on Contributors

Achcar Gilbert is Professor of Development Studies and International Relations at SOAS, University of London.

Yami Bhattarai Manushi is a Nepalese scholar and political activist, and she is teaches rural development in a Tribhuvan University affiliate college in Kathmandu, Nepal.

Bunwaree Sheila is a scholar activist and a Professor at the University of Mauritius, Mauritius.

Christiansen Christian Olaf is an associate professor at Aarhus University, and the principal investigator of 'An Intellectual History of Global Inequality, 1960–2015'. He is an intellectual historian who focuses on global inequality, poverty, the United Nations, human rights, and ideas about the role of business in society. His publications include *Progressive Business: An Intellectual History of the Role of Business in Society* (Oxford University Press 2015) and the co-edited volume *Histories of Global Inequality* (Palgrave 2019). Christian has twice been awarded a Sapere Aude grant from Independent Research Fund Denmark, and currently has a Carlsberg Foundation Monograph Fellowship.

Cosovschi Agustín is a historian. His research deals with the political and intellectual history of the Cold War, primarily in South East Europe. He is currently based in Athens and works as a scientific researcher at the Ecole française d'Athènes. He completed his Ph.D. at the École des Hautes Études en Sciences Sociales in France and the University of San Martin in Argentina. Agustín's essay records a captivating personal journey. From being a politically active student during the pink tide wave in Latin America after the turn of the millennium, he started to study Marxism, dependency theory and other strands of critical political economy to explain inequality and injustice. Agustín's essay elegantly shows the juncture between personal experiences and theory.

Dara Krishna Swamy is a political scientist and teaches political theory and comparative politics. at Jamia Millia Islamia University, India.

Ewinyu Arabo K. is an economist working at the Southern Centre for Inequality Studies, a research unit situated at the University of the Witwatersrand in South Africa.

Galbraith James K. holds the Lloyd M. Bentsen, Jr Chair in government/business relations at the Lyndon B. Johnson School of Public Affairs, The University of Texas at Austin, USA.

Greig Alastair is an Emeritus Fellow in Sociology at the Australian National University in Canberra, Australia, and former Head of School of Social Sciences.

Machado-Guichon Mélanie Lindbjerg is a Ph.D. fellow at the Department of Philosophy and History of Ideas at Aarhus University. Trained in the fields of Anthropology and International Studies, her work primality focuses on Ghanaian and African intellectual history and ideas about inequality as well as, more broadly, the relationship between positionality and thought, centring primarily on post-independence Ghana. Melanie's Ph.D. project explores how Ghanaian intellectuals, since independence in 1957, have conceptualised and vocabularised global inequality and the idea of an unequal world in different contexts and debates.

Hunt Oliver Bugge is a Ph.D. fellow at the Department of Food and Resource Economics, Copenhagen University. He is B.A. in political philosophy, M.A. in conflict and environment analysis from Aarhus University, and holds an M.Sc. in political economy and globalisation from SOAS University of London. Drawing on political economy, science and technology studies, and geography, his research focuses on climate and energy politics in a European context. He is currently working on a project about the changing role of gas infrastructure when countries seek to decarbonise their economies.

Jha Priyanka is an assistant professor of political science, Banaras Hindu University, India. Her research interests lie in gendered intellectual history, political theory, and political thought in modern India. Most recently, she has been awarded the Dr. D. C. Pavate Visiting fellowship at University of Cambridge. She is affiliated with the Department of Politics and International Studies (POLIS) and Sidney Sussex College. She will be working on her project '*Women thinking the world: An Intellectual history of India and South Asia*'. Priyanka is also finishing her manuscript '*Thinking and Ideas that shaped Bharat: Political Thought in Modern India*'.

Kho Tung-Yi is a Research Fellow at the Centre of Cultural Research and Development at Lingnan University in Hong Kong.

Kvangraven Ingrid Harvold is Lecturer in International Development at King's College, London, UK.

Li Tania Murray is Professor of Anthropology at the University of Toronto, Canada.

McClure Julia is Lecturer in late medieval and early modern global history at the University of Glasgow, Scotland.

Menon Dilip is a historian of ideas, the Mellon Chair in Indian Studies, and the Director of the Centre for Indian Studies in Africa at the University of Witwatersrand, South Africa.

Mercader Sofía is a postdoctoral researcher at Aarhus University. Her work primarily focuses on Argentine and Latin American intellectual culture, left-wing intellectuals, and Latin American feminism. She holds a Ph.D. in Hispanic Studies from the University of Warwick and a B.A. in Philosophy from the University of Buenos Aires. She is the author of '*Punto de Vista' and the Argentine Intellectual Left* (Palgrave Macmillan, 2021), A historical study of the Argentine cultural magazine *Punto de Vista* (1978–2008). From 2019 to 2020, she was a postdoctoral researcher at the National Autonomous University of Mexico.

Mignolo Walter is William Hane Wannamaker Distinguished Professor of Romance Studies at Duke University, USA.

Milanovic Branko is a Senior Scholar at the Stone Center on Socioeconomic Inequality, The Graduate Center, City University of New York.

Shankar S. is a novelist, cultural critic and translator, and Professor of English at the University of Hawai'i at Mānoa.

Stuurman Siep is Emeritus Professor of the History of Ideas at Utrecht University, The Netherlands.

Therborn Göran is a global social scientist of Swedish roots and Professor Emeritus of Sociology at the University of Cambridge, UK.

Vergara Camila is a critical legal theorist, historian, and journalist from Chile, and a Marie Skłodowska-Curie Fellow at the University of Cambridge, UK.

LIST OF FIGURES

The Crisis of Neoliberal Capitalism

Landscapes of Hierarchy

Experiences of Inequality from India, a Sociobiographical View

Global Resistances and Solidarities: A View from Nepal

From Chile to New York City: Systemic Corruption and Oligarchic Domination

Making the Familiar Strange: Anthropological Reflections

Introduction: Talking About Global Inequality

*Christian Olaf Christiansen, Sofía Mercader,
Mélanie Lindbjerg Machado-Guichon, Oliver Bugge Hunt,
and Priyanka Jha*

Talking about Global Inequality is a book of interview essays with nineteen public intellectuals and scholars from all over the world reflecting on some of the biggest questions of our age: what is global inequality, what causes it and how should we deal with it? By reading their responses to

––––––––––––

C. O. Christiansen (✉) · S. Mercader · M. L. Machado-Guichon
Aarhus University, Aarhus, Denmark
e-mail: idecoc@cas.au.dk

S. Mercader
e-mail: smercader@cas.au.dk

M. L. Machado-Guichon
e-mail: mlg@cas.au.dk

O. B. Hunt
University of Copenhagen, Copenhagen, Denmark
e-mail: obh@ifro.ku.dk

P. Jha
Banaras Hindu University, Varanasi, India
e-mail: priyaankajha@gmail.com

these questions, we learn how the contributors' personal background, and the places they have worked and lived, have shaped their views on global inequality, a topic they all engage with in their professional, academic lives. We learn about the causes of global inequality, the historical factors that have shaped the world into an unequal place, and the challenges that humanity is confronted with in the face of the widening gap between the poor and the rich. This book aims at showing that thinking about and discussing global inequality demands us to learn about how this long-lasting phenomenon is and has been experienced, and thought of, in different countries across all continents. The contributors to this book all offer their own viewpoints and theories in connection to their personal experiences and background by answering five key questions:

1. What is your background and how did you become interested in global inequality?
2. What is global inequality?
3. How have the places in which you have lived and worked influenced your view on global inequality?
4. What are the main historical causes of global inequality?
5. What are the most pressing contemporary challenges concerning global inequality, and how do we deal with them?

With the aim of including as many perspectives as possible, accommodating both very known and lesser known individuals as well as different genders and age groups, the invitation to participate in this book was partly premised on the contributors' geographical area of expertise, country of birth and nationality. The author's home-discipline was also a factor we considered in the selection process. Readers will be able to discover myriad viewpoints on the question of global inequality, as interviewees are experts in disciplines ranging from history to economics, philosophy to sociology, literary studies to anthropology, intellectual history to political science. Hence, we hope to demonstrate that the topic of global inequality can be approached from multiple angles, both quantitative and qualitative, and that each perspective has something valuable to say on its causes and effects. By doing so, this book aims at transcending the traditional boundaries between research and research dissemination, between our interest in the past and our interest in the present.

Global inequality is one of the most pressing issues of our time. Many social protests and uprisings over the last two decades have been against austerity, socioeconomic grievances, racism, sexism, caste and class based discriminations, disparity in who causes and who suffers from climate change and other forms of human misery and hardship. From the late 1990s global justice movement to the Arab Spring, from Occupy Wall Street to anti-austerity movements in Europe and elsewhere in the wake of the 2008 financial crisis, economic inequalities and insecurities have brought protestors to the streets. Between 2018 and 2019, with a peak in the autumn of 2019, protests against social reforms, costly social services, low wages, defunding public services, precarious work conditions, austerity and more took place in countries including Argentina, Belgium, Chile, Colombia, Ecuador, Egypt, France, Honduras, Lebanon, Nicaragua, Sudan, Taiwan and Zimbabwe. From the #MeToo movement to Black Lives Matter, the twenty-first century bears witness to continuing illegitimate gender and racial inequalities. From Oxfam reporting on extreme wealth inequality to the 2019 *Human Development Report* on global inequality, and from the current global pandemic and global vaccination inequality, highlighting power hierarchies and geographical discrepancies, to the intimate relationships between climate change and inequalities, global inequality is—and is very likely to remain—a main theme well into the twenty-first century.

Studies of global inequality have surged in the social sciences and the humanities in the last couple of decades. The term is now used in fields such as global health, climate change, citizenship, gender, migration, water access, international institutions, macroeconomics and international trade.[1] A similar interest is seen in sociology, anthropology, moral philosophy and epidemiology. Research on inequality has proliferated within economics, especially after the 2008 financial crisis. Historical research on global inequality has focused on measurement, multiple dimensions, institutions, capitalism, politics and deep historical explanations for global inequality and equalization. A good expression of the spectacular surge in the interest in global inequality is the broad success, beyond the

---

[1] For an overview of research on global inequality, see Christian Olaf Christiansen and Steven L. B. Jensen, "Histories of Global Inequality: Introduction," in *Histories of Global Inequality: New Perspectives*, eds. Christian Olaf Christiansen and Steven L. B. Jensen (Palgrave Macmillan, 2019), 1–31. Open access: https://link.springer.com/chapter/10.1007/978-3-030-19163-4_1

confines of academic circles, of books by prominent economists such as Naila Kabeer, Branko Milanovic, Thomas Piketty and Amartya Sen. Their books, and their widespread popularization, bring testimony to a broad and growing interest in the topic of global inequality.

However, the mapping of global inequality would be limited and parsimonious if due attention is not given to the historical contextual dimension. As shown in this book, the concept of global inequality can be and has been articulated through different languages and context-specific concepts that emphasize the importance of a historical contextual understanding of this problem and the urgency of its resolution. *Talking about Global Inequality* brings forward viewpoints that are not limited to economics but, rather, come from multiple disciplines. Moreover, the interview essays not only spring from different disciplinary backgrounds, but are also shaped by diverse geographies, as contributors were born and have lived in all four corners of the world. This collection of interview essays gives readers the opportunity to reflect upon global inequality from multiple perspectives and viewpoints through the manifold voices brought forth in the following pages. In so doing, *Talking about Global Inequality* provides a fruitful and stimulating supplement to a burgeoning area of popular research literature.

A basic premise of this book is that experiences shape people's fields of inquiry and research; that personal backgrounds and the places we grow up or visit are crucial factors in influencing our views and thoughts about the world—in other words, our positionality. Positionality is not only central in shaping one's world view but is also key to one's access to resources and opportunities. Our location in society, in the nation and in the larger global context, influence our lives and our decisions.[2] The interest in the relationship between place and thought and the ambition to include diverse voices, which lies at the base of this book, springs, inter alia, from another fundamental challenge of our times: the need to decolonize academia. This is an agenda which seeks to include previously marginalized and muted voices and diversify the 'canon' and the narratives, perspectives and theories which we are usually presented with—mainly based on the point of view of the hegemonic and unmarked position of the white, European male.

---

[2] For an insightful argument on how our understanding of the world is guided by our experience see Charles Taylor, *Sources of the Self: The Making of Modern Identity* (Cambridge: Cambridge University Press, 1989).

The calls to decolonize the university were made particularly visible in March 2015 when student protests at the University of Cape Town, South Africa, demanded the removal of the statue of the British imperialist and colonial politician Cecil John Rhodes (1853–1902) placed on Campus and brought further attention to the need to decolonize the university as an institution. These protests spread to other places in the world and like other global movements such as Black Lives Matter and #Metoo, as mentioned above, brought to light persisting global inequalities and power hierarchies of today's world.

Recent demands to decolonize knowledge and the production hereof nonetheless stand on the shoulders of a long history of resistance, struggle and contestation such as the anti-colonial struggle throughout the Global South during the mid-twentieth century, the civil rights movement in the US as well as academic critiques formed within fields such as postcolonial and subaltern studies and gender history, to mention a few, emerging during the 1970s and 1980s. In a similar vein, feminist scholars during the 1980s formulated the foundations of 'feminist standpoint theory.' Knowledge was situated and perspectival, argued North American feminist scholars such as Nancy Hartsock, Dorothy Smith and Patricia Hill Collins.[3] In her seminal article, "Situated Knowledges," published in 1988, feminist scholar Donna Haraway similarly emphasized the unavoidable partiality of all knowledge production. The aim, for Haraway, was to challenge and denounce 'the god trick,' denoting the idea that proper knowledge could only be achieved through a disinterested and impartial position, observing 'everything' from 'nowhere.'[4] Instead, knowledge was to be regarded as partial and situated, raising awareness of the importance of the 'politics of location' or what Argentine decolonial

---

[3] See e.g. Nancy Hartsock, "The Feminist Standpoint: Developing the Ground for a Specifically feminist Historical Materialism," in *Discovering Reality*, eds. Sandra Harding and Merill B. Hintikka (Dordrecht: Springer, 1983), 283–310; Patricia Hill Collins, "Learning from the Outsider Within: The Sociological Significance of Black Feminist Thought;" *Social problems* 33, no. 6 (1986): 14–32;

Dorothy Smith, *The Everyday World as Problematic: A Feminist Sociology* (Boston: Northeastern University Press, 1987). See also Sandra Harding, *The Science Question in Feminism* (Milton Keynes: Open University Press, 1986).

[4] Donna Haraway,"Situated Knowledges: The Science Question in Feminism and the Privilege of Partial Perspective," *Feminist studies* 14, no. 13 (1988): 575–599, 581.

scholar Walter Mignolo calls the 'locus of enunciation'—the positionality (both geographical and epistemic) of a person.[5] As Mignolo himself explains in his contribution to this book, the concept of the 'coloniality of power'—which he, along with other Latin American decolonial scholars, defends—points towards the need to acknowledge one's position within the 'colonial matrix of power'—the knowledge hierarchy which, according to Mignolo, shapes the modern world. The category of the subaltern along others such as place, 'race' as well as gender are brought in as important notions in the process of challenging the hegemony of Western knowledge forms by looking towards alternative perspectives generated by different positions and experiences.

This book thus builds on both more recent calls for the need to decolonize the university, its pedagogy, curriculum and knowledge production in general as well as the academic agendas offered by fields such as postcolonial, feminist and decolonial studies. As the world of global inequalities is one of an inequality of voices, this book brings in a heightened focus on the different positionalities and experiences, which to varying degrees and in different ways shape and have shaped the views of the nineteen contributing intellectuals and scholars included in this book. While we do not at all wish to claim that the experiences and the places we have been strictly determine our thoughts and world views, this book insists on the importance of positionality.

Talking about Global Inequality brings in more voices from around the world than we normally hear from. It tells stories about what it means to grow up as a woman in Kenya, what it is like belonging to the lowest caste in India, how it may feel being black or coming from a different ethnic group in Europe or part of a privileged family in Chile. It combines such personal narratives that give us insights into many different countries and cultures around the world, with deep reflections on inequalities as diverse, contemporary and historical phenomena. The book brings in historical experiences and reflections on inequalities in countries as diverse as Australia, Belgium, China, Germany, India, Indonesia, Japan, Kenya, Lebanon, Mauritius, Mozambique, Nepal, The Netherlands, Nigeria, Portugal, Russia, Scotland, Senegal, Singapore, South Africa, Sweden, the US, the Former Republic of Yugoslavia and many more. This helps in

---

[5] Walter Mignolo, *The Darker Side of Western Modernity: Global Futures, Decolonial Options* (Durham: Duke University Press, 2011).

crafting its transnational perspective on global inequality—and makes this a global book on a global topic.

This book, then, is an assembly of such multiple voices. A few snap-shots are presented here to give a feel of the collection of interview essays ahead. Göran Therborn, world-known Swedish sociologist and author of the seminal book *The Killing Fields of Inequality*, puts the matter succinctly when he explains what global inequality is: "Global inequality is the unequal distribution of human life chances in the world. It is multi-dimensional, but on a global scale today it is more than anything else inequality of power, of possibilities of self-determination." In the inter-view, we learn more about what influenced Therborn's perspective: "I grew up in a family of farmers in southeastern Sweden, certainly not cosmopolitan, but my father was interested in world affairs. On my own, I became a life-long anti-imperialist. My first discussion of international politics with my father, at age nine, was on the Korean war."

Therborn is certainly not alone in reflecting upon childhood experi-ences. Indeed, this is something which runs through many contributors' responses when asked about their personal background. In the chapter "From Chile to New York: Systemic Corruption and Oligarchic Domi-nation," Camila Vergara, Chilean critical legal theorist and author of *Systemic Corruption: Constitutional Ideas for an Anti-Oligarchic Republic* (Princeton University Press 2020), takes us back to her childhood experi-ences in Chile: "It was during my first job as assistant *campera* (cowgirl) at the ranch at age 10 that I was confronted with the rigid socioeco-nomic hierarchy that separated me (granddaughter of the *patrón*) from the workers—despite us being equally high on our horses and equally buried, knee-deep in mud and cow muck."

Not surprisingly, another influential factor in shaping people's views is their travelling to other countries. In this regard, many interview essays are as a horn of plenty from which manifold experiences from around the globe continue to flow—and with very different personal experiences of inequality from country to country. As an example, one interview not only takes us to India, Germany and Nigeria, but also to the US mainland as well as Hawaii. S. Shankar, Indian novelist, cultural critic, translator and Professor of English at the University of Hawai'i at Mānoa, nicely captures an experience shared by other contributors when he writes: "Ironically, the privilege of travel has taught me to think comparatively about a global lack of privilege. As a writer I began composing short stories and poems about the poor. Later, poverty and inequality came to be thematized directly in two of my three novels." Or as Siep Stuurman, Emeritus Professor of the History of Ideas at Utrecht University and author of *The Invention of Humanity* (Harvard University Press, 2017), states in his contribution: "When I first spent some months in New York in 1988, I was shocked by the amount of destitution, poverty, dirt and homelessness on the streets of the most magnificent city in what I then believed to be the richest country in the world."

Yet, if childhood memories as well as travelling are crucial in nurturing peoples' interest and their thinking on inequalities, history is a major source of inspiration too. This becomes evident when Julia McClure, lecturer in late medieval and early modern global history at the University of Glasgow, and founder of the Poverty Research Network, explains her route into working on global inequality: "My work on the Franciscans led to my understanding of the role that beliefs and institutions play in the justifications of the forms of inequality that develop with global empires and global capitalism."

1   ORGANIZATION

This book is divided into four main sections. While we encourage you to read the essays in this book in the order you find most interesting, the four parts provide one possible way of reading through the included interview essays.

Part I, "Deep Roots: Legacies of Imperialism and Colonialism," encloses five interview essays which in different ways address the deep historical roots of global inequalities. In these five essays, authored by Siep Stuurman, Julia McClure, Göran Therborn, Walter Mignolo and Kho Tung-yi, the imperial and colonial legacy of contemporary inequalities on a global scale are unpacked. Emphasizing slavery and racism during the Enlightenment era, the Spanish empire, the Korean and Vietnam wars, European colonialism and the history of Singapore, these contributions all point to the need for a deep historical perspective on the inequalities of today's world.

The five interview essays written by Branko Milanovic, James K. Galbraith, Alastair Greig, Ingrid Kvangraven and Gilbert Achcar make up Part II of the book, "Unequal Entanglements: A Capitalist World System." Here, the contributors discuss the role of the capitalist world system when trying to understand and deal with today's global inequalities. They highlight the importance of reducing global income and wealth inequality; of understanding the centrality and role of global finance; of listening to and respecting the voices of indigenous peoples, as well as dealing with pressing issues related to climate and environmental changes.

Part III, "The Inertia of Hierarchies: Class, Caste, 'Race', Gender," explores the importance of categories such as class, caste, 'race' and gender when investigating the persistence and experiences of global inequality. The five essays included here by Dilip Menon, Krishna Swamy, S. Shankar, Arabo K. Ewinyu and Manushi Yami Bhattarai all address these categories from different perspectives. They point at the centrality of intersectionality—the intersections of different identities and experiences—when trying to understand how global inequalities are upheld and felt.

The fourth and last part of the book, Part IV, is "Thinking Beyond Economics: The Politics of Inequalities." This part gathers four contributions by Camila Vergara, Tania Murray Li, Agustín Cosovschi and Sheila Bunwaree. These essays engage with different aspects of the politics of inequalities, and how inequalities have been legitimized and reproduced through law or through grand narratives such as "progress" and "development." As a way of transcending the fabrication of inequalities, these essays invite us to think beyond economics. They highlight the need to focus on climate justice, ending orthodox economics obsession with GDP growth, and developing alternative economies that integrate environmental limits, inclusion, fairness and equity.

The making of these interview essays has included several steps. Contributors have written their answers to our five questions, after which they have typically been through three rounds of editing. We have aimed at a non-intrusive editing process where we asked interviewees to elaborate, specify and exemplify rather than 'forcing through' their statements on particular issues. We also tried to keep references at a minimum. Some chapters are accompanied by photos, all taken by interviewees themselves, with the aim of giving readers a sense of some of the many different places referred to in the essays.

We hope this book will offer a unique room for reflection on our present predicament in a world of extreme global inequality. It aspires to give readers an opportunity to ponder about different contemporary inequalities from around the world. With this book, we learn how key experts and intellectuals themselves came to think about inequalities in particular ways, and to understand the much larger historical contexts and dynamics of present-day inequalities. Combining personal stories and local histories with global concerns, sharp analyses of current affairs with an eye to the deep impacts of historical forces, our aim has been a book that is both academic, political and highly contemporary. We hope *Talking about Global Inequality* may help us all understand and engage with other worlds, to open our communities to others, and to extend our solidarity against global inequality as a common struggle.

Deep Roots: Legacies of Imperialism and Colonialism

Notes for a New History

Siep Stuurman

1 What is Your Background and How Did You Become Interested in Global Inequality?

I am an intellectual historian, and my starting point was the history of equality. In the 1980s and 1990s, when I taught the history of political thought at the University of Amsterdam, feminist students demanded the inclusion of woman authors in the syllabus. I responded by delivering a series of six two-hour lectures on Mary Wollstonecraft, the British champion of women's rights. To contextualize her feminism, I had to retrieve the discourses of male supremacy and the subjection of women. The French philosopher Jean-Jacques Rousseau, a favorite butt of Wollstonecraft's critique, provided the means to insert early modern feminism in the canon of the history of political thought, in particular because Rousseau himself had defended the equality of the sexes as a young man (from the 1730s to ca. 1748).

In the mid-1990s, I began a research project on François Poulain de la Barre, a Cartesian social philosopher who in 1673 published

S. Stuurman (✉)
History of Ideas, Utrecht University, Utrecht, Netherlands
e-mail: S.Stuurman@uu.nl

C. O. Christiansen et al. (eds.), *Talking About Global Inequality*,
https://doi.org/10.1007/978-3-031-08042-5_2

13

A Physical and Moral Discourse on the Equality of the two Sexes, in which one sees the importance of getting rid of prejudices. Let me quote one sentence to give you the flavor of the argument: "Popular views hold that Turks, barbarians, and savages are less adept at [learning] than Europeans. Nevertheless, should five or six of them turn up with this ability, or with a doctorate […] this opinion would be definitely corrected, and we would concede that these peoples are human beings like us, with the same abilities."[1] Here, we encounter a truly universalist discourse of equality, covering gender, rank, and cultural difference.[2]

Working on the Poulain book, I became more and more dissatisfied with the canon of the history of political thought. It was a Eurocentric collection of "great thinkers" and its linchpin was the history of liberty. Equality was mentioned from time to time, but it was definitely the stepchild of the canon. Moreover, I was surprised by the virtual absence of book-length treatments of the history of equality.[3] So I decided to write the missing book myself. To avoid getting mired in a "history of everything," I focused on the problematic of cultural difference. At that time, around 2006, a committee of historians appointed by the Dutch government published a new canon for the teaching of national history in elementary schools and high-schools. I was among its critics. I argued for a world-historical approach to revise and reframe our national history in its global connections, in an essay published by *Kleio*, the review of the Dutch Association of History Teachers. With my Rotterdam colleague Maria Grever, I edited a book about the canon-debates.[4] The controversy about the history syllabus was part of broader acrimonious debate

---

[1] François Poulain de la Barre, *De l'égalité des deux sexes, discours physique et moral, où l'on voit l'importance de se défaire des préjugés* ([1673] Paris: Fayard, 1984), 38 (my translation).

[2] Also see Siep Stuurman, *François Poulain de la Barre and the Invention of Modern Equality* (Cambridge, Mass. & London: Harvard University Press, 2004).

[3] Siep Stuurman, "The Canon of the History of Political Thought: Its Critique and a Proposed Alternative," *History and Theory*, 39 (2000): 147–166.

[4] Maria Grever and Siep Stuurman (eds.), *Beyond the Canon: History for the Twenty-first Century* (Basingstoke & New York: Palgrave Macmillan, 2007).

about the significance of the nation between left-wing critics of the traditional nationalist narrative and right-wing populists. All of these inputs went into the writing of my book *The Invention of Humanity*.[5]

2   What is Global Inequality?

I would like to reframe the question and ask instead: When, where, by whom, and why was global inequality put on the political and intellectual agenda? The shortest answers to the first three questions I can think of are: in the eighteenth century, in the trans-Atlantic space, by the enslaved Africans and by a minority of white Europeans. The eighteenth-century controversies about slavery present us with the first instance of a debate about global inequality.

The question about the "why" is not so easily answered. The traditional justifications of slavery slowly lost their credibility, but this was a highly uneven and contested affair that would last deep into the nineteenth and twentieth century. Several ex-slaves residing in Europe published life-stories that recounted the horrors of slavery, the longing for freedom and several of them demanded its abolition. In the white camp, several political theorists spoke out against slavery. The French scholar Louis de Jaucourt, the workhorse of French philosopher Rene Diderot (of the 72,000 entries in the *Encyclopedia*, Jaucourt signed 17,000) authored the entry on equality as a concept of natural right, defining it as the equality "that is found among all men solely by the constitution of their nature."[6] In another entry, on the slave trade, he declared that the capture of black Africans to sell them into slavery "violates religion, morals, natural law and all the rights of human nature." This is strong language, but it stops short of abolitionism.

Generally, the eighteenth-century white debates on slavery are uneven and contradictory. Another influential French philosopher, Montesquieu, is an instructive example. In the thousand pages of annotations and comments that he always had on his desk, he stated that the war waged

[5] Siep Stuurman, *The Invention of Humanity: Equality and Cultural Difference in World History* (Cambridge Mass. & London: Harvard University Press, 2017).

[6] Louis de Jaucourt, "égalité (droit naturel)," in *Encyclopédie ou dictionnaire raisonné des sciences, des arts et des métiers*, réd. Denis Diderot and Jean le Rond d'Alembert (Paris 1751–1772), 5: 415. References are to the online ARTFL Encyclopédie Project: https://encyclopedie.uchicago.edu/

by the Roman slave rebellion leader Spartacus was the "most just war in the history of humanity," but that comment did not make it to the pages of the *Spirit of the Laws* (1748).[7] What we find there is an ironical dismissal of slavery, but not a vindication of its overthrow by armed slaves. However, French Enlightenment writers Guillaume Thomas Raynal and Diderot, in the *Histoire des deux Indes* (1780), one of the great bestsellers of the late Enlightenment, countenanced the violent overthrow of slavery. They voiced their expectations of a new Spartacus who would "shatter the sacrilegious yoke of oppression."[8] In the same period, the American, French, and Haitian revolutions created the first states in human history which enshrined equality in their constitutions. This was a world-historical turning point: Henceforth, equality had the benefit of the doubt, while inequality had to be justified by reasonable arguments.

Even so, the nineteenth century entrenched the global color line that only became disreputable after the defeat of Nazi Germany. But racism did not disappear. Today, we witness a new upsurge of it, despite the civil rights victories in the United States and the decolonization of Africa. This is a dimension of global inequality that time and again seems to fade away, only to rise again from its ashes. Race is transposed onto the cultural superiority of "the West" and anchored in a genetic determinism (the "selfish gene") that has meanwhile been deconstructed by the new theoretical venture of "systems biology."[9] Of course, global inequality also has economic foundations to which I will come back in question four.

3   How Have the Places in Which You Have Lived and Worked Influenced Your View on Global Inequality?

When I first spent some months in New York in 1988, I was shocked by the amount of destitution, poverty, dirt, and homelessness on the streets

---

[7] Montesquieu, *Pensées / Le Spicilège*, ed. Louis Desgraves (Paris: Robert Laffont, 1991), 228.

[8] Guillaume Thomas Raynal, *Histoire philosophique et politique des établissements et du commerce des Européens dans les deux Indes*, 10 vols (Geneva: Jean-Leonard Pellet, 1782), VI: 138–139.

[9] Denis Noble, *The Music of Life: Biology Beyond Genes* (Oxford & New York: Oxford University Press, 2006).

of the most magnificent city in what I then believed to be the richest country in the world. At home in Europe, we were already living through the first spate of spending cuts in welfare and social services, but that was peanuts compared with New York.

Likewise "race" and racism were far more visible. I still vividly remember taking the train to Princeton and noticing what was printed on my ticket: "Seating aboard New Jersey Transit vehicles is without regard to race, creed, color or national origin." That an American railway felt the need to put that on their tickets told me something about the over-whelming presence of race more than 120 years after the Civil War. From then on, I took the category of race more seriously. Meanwhile, I enjoyed the openness and intellectual curiosity of American academic life. New York taught me a lot, both intellectually and politically.

Until my stay in New York, my view of worldwide inequality—we did not yet use the term "global"—turned on the contrast between the poor "Third World" and the rich "West." Now, I began to be aware of the existence of raw poverty within the West. I had read a book on Latin America that explained that poor countries also harbored extremely wealthy elites, the "comprador bourgeoisie" as they were then called. The upshot was that henceforth I had to understand that worldwide inequality could only be analyzed as a composite of wealth and income differentials within and between countries.

Some twelve years later, I spent some months at University of California, Los Angeles (UCLA). In Westwood where I lived in L.A., many white people had nice homes with large gardens. On the streets I noticed cars of a security company. Those cars were driven by imposing African-American men, but the gardeners who mowed the lawns were mostly Latinos. At the university, however, many secretaries were Asian-American women. Here was a distinct pattern. What I learned was that race and racism were not just about individual prejudices but should also, and perhaps primarily, be investigated as organizing principles of a society.

4   What Are the Main Historical Causes of Global Inequality?

Before ca. 1750 CE, the economic disparities between continents, regions, and countries were not spectacular. Parts of the world were much richer than the average, but these rich "islands" were not concentrated in the "West," they were also found in Bengal and in the Yangtze Delta in China, and probably elsewhere as well. As the economic historian Paul Bairoch concludes: "Before the Industrial Revolution no country or region could be really rich [...] Richer regions of the future Third World appear to have been richer than the average countries in the future developed world, and vice versa."[10]

After 1750, and even more after 1800, the growth in productivity, both in agriculture and in manufacturing, accelerated quickly, notably in the Atlantic rim of Europe and in the United States. Between 1800 and 2000, the gap between the "West" and the "rest" continuously grew wider. The explanation cannot be found in the pre-1750/1800 patterns of growth. I can think of three explanations. First, the growth of productivity in the West, based on technology market competition, and "productive" state intervention (think railways, roads, bridges). Second, the adverse effects of the forced liberalization of trade imposed by the West on the economic development of countries of the future Third World. The West gained new export markets, but the producers in the "less developed countries" lost a sizable chunk of their internal markets. And third, the counter-productive activities of predator-states where elites were keener on conspicuous consumption than on productive investments.

5   What Are the Most Pressing Contemporary Challenges Concerning Global Inequality, and How Do We Deal with Them?

Without doubt, the most pressing challenge is the accelerating increase of economic inequality within and between nations diagnosed by Thomas Piketty. The new type of inequality is not only about increasing destitution and poverty but also, and perhaps primarily, about the crippling effects of neo-liberalism on the tax base of states. The great multinational corporations, high finance, and the super-rich are morphing into a new Global Aristocracy. This is a gold-blooded caste which manages the key sectors of the world economy, pressures states to lower taxes on an ad-hoc basis, sluices profits to tax havens, and lobbies for commercial treaties with special tribunals for Investor-State conflicts, thus bypassing ordinary

---

[10] Paul Bairoch, *Economics and World History: Myths and Paradoxes* (New York & London: Harvester Wheatsheaf, 1993).

courts of law. Many of these new Aristocrats live in compounds where they stay physically isolated from ordinary citizens (except for servants and prostitutes).

Right now, I must admit that I don't know how to deal with this huge and growing global inequality. Meanwhile, I am working on a global intellectual history of socio-economic and political equality and inequality, from antiquity to the present time. I will report back when the time has come.

Poverty and Ideology: Historic Pathways

Julia McClure

1   WHAT IS YOUR BACKGROUND AND HOW DID YOU BECOME INTERESTED IN GLOBAL INEQUALITY?

My first research interest was in the socio-religious movement that emerged in reaction to the emergence of the market society and monetisation taking place in Italy in the thirteenth century. This movement, which became the religious institution known as the Franciscan Order, rhetorically rejected market economics while simultaneously contributing to its legitimation within the framework of Christian ethics. The Franciscans developed an ideology of poverty which posited an alternative theory of value to that emerging with capitalism in the late medieval and early modern periods. They imagined a world unified by a material poverty but structured by a spiritual hierarchy in which they were spiritual leaders. They developed a reputation as spiritually powerful and consequently received many donations which made them, paradoxically,

J. McClure (✉)
Senior Lecturer in Late Medieval and Early Modern Global History, University of Glasgow, Glasgow, Scotland
e-mail: Julia.McClure@glasgow.ac.uk

C. O. Christiansen et al. (eds.), *Talking About Global Inequality*,
https://doi.org/10.1007/978-3-031-08042-5_3

materially rich. They justified this wealth by seeing themselves as arbitrators of a spiritual economy, whereby they were custodians of possessions ceded by the laity as gifts to God in return to the 'treasures in heaven' of eternal salvation. In my first monograph, *The Franciscan Invention of the New World*, I examined their role in the creation of the colonial society and in shaping the power dynamics of early globalisation, and in a recent article I argued that the Franciscans envisioned a world connected by a unifying but unequal notion of poverty.[1] My work on the Franciscans led to my understanding of the role that beliefs and institutions play in the justifications of the forms of inequality that develop with global empires and global capitalism.

This informs my current book project, provisionally entitled *Empire of Poverty: The Moral Economy of the Spanish Empire*. The book explores how beliefs about the deserving and underserving poor and moral order were used to construct the socio-racial hierarchies of newly emerging colonial societies; how beliefs about the social function of property and spiritual values of exchange created an institutional landscape where economic exchanges were embedded within socio-cultural processes; and how paternalistic beliefs about providing for the poor undergirded both an authoritarian ideology of governance and a dynamic system of claims to access resources. My work contends that ideology, beliefs, and moral economies shape patterns of inequality.

During my postdoctoral fellowship at Harvard's Weatherhead Centre for Global History, I became interested in the importance of taking a systematic approach to understanding global processes, especially the ways in which the links between capitalism and colonialism shaped the historic pathways to inequality. During my postdoctoral fellowship at the European University Institute, I developed my interest in interdisciplinary methodologies, recognising the challenges and rewards of examining the same subject from different perspectives. I went on to found the Poverty Research Network, which has forged new forms of interdisciplinary approaches to poverty, considering in particular the roles of aesthetics and the politics of representation.[2] I have also participated in

---

[1] Julia McClure, *The Franciscan Invention of the New World* (Basingtoke: Palgrave, 2016); Julia McClure, "The Globalization of Franciscan Poverty," *Journal of World History*, 30, no. 3 (2019): 335–362.

[2] https://www.gla.ac.uk/research/az/poverty/ (visited 19 December, 2021).

interdisciplinary collaborations between history, law, economics, and sociology which aim to increase our understanding of the causes of inequality. In one collaboration, we examine the role of constitutions in shaping patterns of inequality,[3] and in another, we investigate the legacies of different taxation regimes.[4] Through the sharing of insights and expertise, interdisciplinary research can deepen and sharpen our understanding of the causes of global inequality. Through the poverty research network, I have developed global conversations on poverty, which have taught me about the different ways that poverty has been conceptualised and perceived at different times and in different societies. These differing conceptions of poverty that have existed in different times and in different places point towards the real poverty of values which is at the core of the capitalist system. Transforming the value regime that governs the capitalist system is central to addressing questions of global inequality (Fig. 1).

2   What is Global Inequality?

We know that we live in a vastly unequal world. According to the Institute of Policy Studies, the world's richest 1 per cent, those with more than $1 million, own 45 per cent of the world's wealth.[5] Economics has dominated inequality studies, shaping what we know about global inequality. Economic indicators are useful, helping to identify regions of abject poverty and inequality. Since 2010, the UN development programme has incorporated the multidimensional poverty index, and the UN has a definition which includes 'access to education and other basic services, social discrimination and exclusion, as well as the lack of participation in decision-making'.[6] While understandings and definitions of poverty have broadened in the last decades, available macro-data for assessing global inequality tends to rely either on aggregate GDP data or upon income or wealth distribution. Over-reliance on economic indicators of

---

[3] Anna Chadwick, Javier Solana, Eleonora Lozano Rodriguez, Andrés Palacios eds, in *Markets, Constitutions, and Inequality* (Routledge, 2022).

[4] Gurminder K. Bhambra and Julia McClure eds, *Imperial Inequalities: The Politics of Economic Governance across European Empires* (Manchester University Press, expected 2022).

[5] https://inequality.org/facts/global-inequality/#global-wealth-inequality (visited 19th December 2021).

[6] https://www.un.org/en/sections/issues-depth/poverty/

Fig. 1 Building in Rio de Janeiro, Brazil showing graffiti building in foreground and more affluent skyscrapers in background (Photograph taken by Julia McClure)

inequality risk flattening the contours of global inequality and obscuring its social, political, and cultural dimensions. Global inequalities are also racial, gendered, and classed. Multidimensional measures and representations of global inequality must find a way to account for the ways in which inequalities are structured and experienced intersectionally.

There is another problem with leaving economics to define inequality, and that is that large parts of the discipline of economics is underpinned by the ideology and normative assumptions of liberalism and neoliberalism. Classical and neoclassical economics both emphasise the importance of individualised economic growth, which they see as predicated upon the naturalisation of the market in society. New Institutional Economics expands this logic to demonstrate how institutions and laws which protect private property and the right of individuals to make a profit facilitate economic growth. The predominance of economic models enables global inequality to be defined according to a certain cosmos of values. Without interdisciplinary critique of the ideological premises of certain forms of economic analysis, and a broadening of perspective to understand the role that laws and institutions play in enabling the capitalist market system to create inequalities, there will always be a poverty of perspective.

From space, the globe appears as a contiguous unit, with land masses joined by the same seas, hanging under the same skies. Zoom in and you see that the globe is fractured into competing political units, many of which take the form of nation-states. Local conditions shape the characteristics of global inequality. Nation-states and their policies still matter. The global does not erase the local, but rather the two sets of conditions interact to shape patterns of inequality.

3   How Have the Places You Have Lived and Worked Influenced Your View on Global Inequality?

With the Poverty Research Network, I have worked in Senegal, Brazil, and Mexico, all of which are on the ODA (Official Development Assistance) country list, classed as lower- or middle-income countries. Countries that are notable for their wealth inequality in relation to other countries, often have high levels of inequality also within the country. In Senegal, Brazil, and Mexico, a high proportion of income is spent on private security to guard private wealth, and often this investment in private security is driven by fear of high levels of poverty juxtaposed with pockets of relative wealth. This has made me think about the current condition of nation states, and the way in which sovereignty and power are, in reality, fractured into private units that are below the surface of the state. This realisation sparked my interest in early modern corporate constitutionalism, the way in which private trading companies and businesses expanded both empire and capitalism by being awarded privileges which were effectively a kind of franchising of sovereignty.[7] From this

---

[7] The idea of corporate constitutionalism comes from Will Pettigrew, "The Public Rivalry between Regulated and Joint Stock Corporations and the Development of Seventeenth-Century Corporate Constitutions," *Historical Research*, 90, no. 248 (2017): 341–362. For my discussion on the relationship between the public and the private in the colonial process see Julia McClure, 'Conquest by contract: property rights and the commercial logic of imperialism in the Isthmus of Tehuantepec (Southern Mexico)', *Bulletin of Latin American Studies* (2022), and Julia McClure 'Taxation, welfare, and

perspective, we can start to understand global inequality as the product of the blurred boundaries between the public and the private. If we are to understand the historic pathways of inequality, we need to understand the complex ways in which sovereignty is fragmented and can be cannibalised and operationalised away from the common good to advance private interests.

My work on global poverty has taught me that poverty is conceptualised in different ways in different times and in different places and that it often reflect different value systems. International institutions often define poverty in terms of economic indicators of growth and the consumption of certain commodities. Prioritisation of these capitalist indicators often erases local values. For example, many indigenous communities have different ways of valuing the natural world within their epistemological and cosmological schemas.[8] The way that indigenous communities experience inequalities may not be in terms of their reduced purchasing power or commodity consumption but the erasure of their values. Rather than being 'empowered' to operate more efficiently within the market, indigenous communities would suffer fewer inequalities if there were more limitations on commercial expansion and industrial production in and around indigenous territories (Fig. 2).

4   WHAT ARE THE MAIN HISTORICAL CAUSES OF GLOBAL INEQUALITY?

It is hard to deny that the world is characterised by inequality, but there is less consensus around its causes. For years, it was assumed that the wealth disparity was somehow natural, the result of European exceptionalism, or an 'European miracle'. Protagonists of European exceptionalism posited that global inequality was historically caused by the unprecedented trends of economic growth that fitfully began in the sixteenth century and became sustained from the nineteenth century and were the result of endogenous European factors. The global turn has demonstrated that European economic growth which drove global inequality

the inequalities of the Spanish imperial state', in Bhambra and McClure eds, *Imperial Inequalities: The Politics of Economic Governance across European Empires* (Manchester University Press, 2022).

[8] Julia McClure, 'Scarcity and Risk in the Tropics', History Workshop Online (2022), https://www.historyworkshop.org.uk/scarcity-and-risk-in-the-tropics/

Fig. 2 Black and white photo showing archaeology of slave ship port in downtown Rio de Janeiro, Brazil (Photograph taken by Julia McClure)

trends from the sixteenth century to the mid-twentieth century, were not driven by endogenous European factors, but by the global context of European imperialism. Global history has taught us that the poverty of the Global South and the wealth of the Global North are intrinsically connected through the history of imperialism. The global turn demonstrates that the context of colonialism is critical to any understanding of the long-term causes of global inequalities.

We are now over two decades into the global historical turn, and approaches to the historic causes of global inequality continue to branch in new directions. The global history of capitalism is generating new insights into the ways in which the capitalist system and the global inequality it engenders have been made possible by the colonial appropriation of resources and labour. The conjoined processes of capitalism and colonialism have hardwired economic and racial inequalities into the world system. Mapping the way in which this happened is important to processes of decolonisation. Global intellectual history is also important to deepening our understanding of the historic causes of inequalities as we seek to understand the roles that beliefs and ideologies have played in governing human actions and legitimating inequality regimes.[9] How have people imagined what is equal or fair? How have they rationalised and justified what is not? What do different societies value? How is access to the things that people value mediated across different groups? It is important to understand the social and cultural processes in which actions are embedded if we are to slice into the problem of global inequality and place the rich tissue of historical causality under the microscope.

5   WHAT ARE THE MOST PRESSING CONTEMPORARY CHALLENGES CONCERNING GLOBAL INEQUALITY AND HOW DO WE DEAL WITH THEM?

In the wake of the pandemic, many people are re-imagining the future of global inequality. But transformations of the patterns of global inequality will not happen naturally. They must be created through both the imagining of alternate ways of living and ordering society and through the creation of the governing structures and popular consensus that will enable change to take place.

The combined and conjoined pressures of climate change and capitalism will continue to shape the contours of global inequality. To address the problem of global inequality will require systemic change, away from the fetishisation of economic growth, the cycles of over-production and over-consumption, and an ideological shift away from belief in the invisible hand of the market as a naturalised solution to the complexities of exchange. We are increasingly conscious that human societies have surpassed the ecological limits of economic growth. We need to re-imagine an economic model that fulfils social needs without surpassing environmental limitations. This requires systemic change, changing the codes of our laws and institutions, and ideological change, to bring about a revolution of value.

The capitalist system has operated through transforming humans' conception of basic needs to include an increasingly wider range of commodities and through the increased commodification of all aspects of daily life. From the sixteenth century, the expansion of capitalism and

---

[9] see Julia McClure, 'The intellectual foundations of imperial concepts of inequality', Journal of Global Intellectual History (2022).

colonialism went hand in hand as more of the natural world of colonised regions was placed into the stream of commodities for the commercial benefit of colonising nations. To create more equal societies in the future, we must address both the legacies of colonialism that have created not only inequalities between countries but also racial inequalities between peoples, and the legacies of capitalism which have created inequalities between human societies and the natural world.

Ending global inequalities requires a revolution of values driven by the de-commodification of the natural world and a shift of shared conceptions of human needs away from commodities. The possibility of future global equality requires both less capitalistic and less anthropocentric social and economic models underpinned by more harmonious relationships with our complex ecological contexts. We need to transform the way we produce and consume, and to re-value the things that are necessary for life. We must move away from predominantly economic metrics of global poverty and inequality, to find a place for social and ecological values. To this end, the ontologies and epistemologies of indigenous people, who have resisted many waves of colonialism to maintain more harmonious agro-ecological practices, can give important lessons. However, it is important that in the rush to find alternate ways of living that we don't participate in the co-option of indigenous ontologies for the green-washing of capitalism. To this extent we must work towards not only a revolution of value, but a transformation of governance, creating space and legitimacy for polycentric governance.

Anti-Imperialism and Digging for the Bases of Power and Privilege

Göran Therborn

1 WHAT IS YOUR BACKGROUND AND HOW DID YOU BECOME INTERESTED IN GLOBAL INEQUALITY?

Globality came before inequality. I grew up in a family of farmers in south-eastern Sweden, certainly not cosmopolitan, but my father was interested in world affairs. On my own, I became a lifelong anti-imperialist. My first discussion of international politics with my father, at age nine, was on the Korean war. I had neither knowledge nor opinion of the origin and stakes of the war, but I was sceptical of the American right to intervene, and of their chances of success. By the time of the first Vietnam war and the siege of Dien-bien-phu in Spring 1954, I was a convinced anti-colonialist, age twelve and a half, following the radio reports of the advance of the Vietnamese. I think it was the arrogance of imperialist and colonial power which struck me and angered me. The Algerian uprising and its ensuing war broke out in November 1954, and I followed it from

G. Therborn (✉)
Sociology, University of Cambridge, Cambridge, UK
e-mail: goran.therborn.extern@lnu.se; gt274@cam.ac.uk

Sociology, Linnaeus University, Växjö-Kalmar, Sweden

C. O. Christiansen et al. (eds.), *Talking About Global Inequality*,
https://doi.org/10.1007/978-3-031-08042-5_4

31

the beginning, in Swedish radio and newspapers. Inequality was something I came to see as deriving from the power of empire and of the class of capital, and the bases and mechanisms of capitalist power, particularly in democratic forms, has been a major research interest. In the 1950s to early 1970s that power did not look invincible, on the contrary. Therefore, most important and most interesting was to study the forces of possible change, anti-imperialist movements, structures and movements of class. That colonialism, imperialism, and capitalism were deeply and viciously unequal was self-evident. When the powers behind inequalities got to look more stable and fortified, the patterns of and the ways and means behind inequality became more salient.

A decisive intellectual influence on me was Amartya Sen's 1988 lecture *Equality of What?*, which I came across a few years later.[1] Inequality mattered above all because it meant unequal capabilities to function fully as a human being. Seen in this way, inequality meant much more than the size of income differences. It meant violations of the most fundamental human rights.

2   What is Global Inequality?

Global inequality is the unequal distribution of human life chances in the world. It is multidimensional, but on a global scale today, it is more than anything else inequality of power, of possibilities of self-determination. Inequality of resources to realize one's hopes of a safe and healthy environment to grow up in and of never having to go hungry, of an education to learn what one would like to do, of getting a meaningful and supporting job, of choosing the partner one loves, of being able to criticize and to try to change what one finds wrong or unjust. The denial to the great majority of humankind of possibilities to realize their potential is the core of global inequality.

Inequality, local, national, and global, has three fundamental dimensions, which may be seen as reflecting the dimensions of what it means to be human.[2]

---

[1] The lecture is included in Amartya Sen, *Inequality Reexamined* (Cambridge, MA: Harvard University Press, 1992), 12–30.

[2] Please see Göran Therborn, *The Killing Fields of Inequality* (Cambridge, UK: Polity, 2013).

Vital inequality, i.e. the socially determined distribution of hunger and malnutrition, of health and ill health, of short and long lifespans.

Existential inequality refers to the conditions of existence of human persons or human selves. Their allocation of emotional security, support and encouragement, recognition and respect, self-confidence, ambitions, freedom, and of their opposites, insecurity and fear, neglect and discouragement, ignorance and humiliation, self-doubt and self-hatred, and existential confinement. Patriarchy, racism, caste, and class are the main manifestations of existential inequality.

Resource inequality is most often discussed in terms of income and wealth. But generally, it also includes power, office, status, or violence, and social assets, whether "contacts" or membership of a community. In specific contexts, a wide variety of resources may be relevant.

The three dimensions are interdependent and interacting, but they are not reducible to each other, and they develop along different trajectories, as do the geographical referent of global and national.

3   How Have the Places You Have Lived and Worked Influenced Your View on Global Inequality?

Periods of international conjunctures have probably influenced me and my views on global inequality more than places. My early student years at Lund were much under the influence of Africa. 1960 was the year of mass independence in Africa, and of the beginning of the first neocolonial reaction to it, the Congo crisis. I started to subscribe to several African newspapers, among them *Accra Evening News, le Soleil* from Dakar and *The Daily Times* from Lagos. By the mid-1960s, African independence had turned into disappointment and disillusion. I became increasingly interested in Latin America. I was invited to the Cultural Congress of Havana in January 1968, an inspiring worldwide gathering of anti-imperialist intellectuals. For a session there, I drafted what became my first international article, *From Petrograd to Saigon*, explaining why the Vietnam war had such a different political impact than the Korean war.[3]

---

[3] Göran Therborn, "From Petrograd to Saigon," *New Left Review* 48 (March 1968): 3–11.

Then came a period in my life shaped by Swedish political engagement for a New Left, followed by scholarly devotion and intercontinental travel.[4] Meanwhile, the Third World darkened with the massacres in Indonesia, the wave of military dictatorships in Latin America and Africa, the Pol Pot regime in Cambodia, and the Chinese attack on Vietnam.

In the 1980s, I was mostly in the Netherlands working on comparative public policy and welfare states, as a sociologist turned professor of political science. In the post-radical 1990s, I was back in Sweden. Europe was in the air, and I wrote a historical sociology of Europe, East and West. Towards the end of the decade, globalization became the buzzword of social analysis. The national interdisciplinary research group I was chairing mutated from European to global studies.

My lifelong egalitarianism has never been rooted in personal humiliation or resentment. Stark economic inequality has for me largely been a visitor's experience, in North Africa in 1963, in Mexico first time in 1974, in India from 1977, in West Africa, Brazil, and Central America from 1978, in Los Angeles in 1991. From 2014, I worked in South Africa, the world's most unequal country, a couple of weeks every year for four years.

4   What Are the Main Historical Causes of Global Inequality?

When unfolding the main historical causes to global inequality, let us start by distinguishing the timescape of the fundamental dimensions of inequality. Life expectancy, taken as a key indicator of vital inequality, seems to start differentiating, among classes as well as among countries, in the second half of the eighteenth century. It is then only that the longevity of English ducal families begin to surge above that of the general population.[5] On a global inter-country scale, substantial "health transitions" to a longer life began in Northwestern Europe in the last decades of the eighteenth century, led by Denmark, Sweden, and France (from a much lower level), followed by England and Wales in the nineteenth century.[6] Better

---

[4] Before 1968 I had, together with a few pals, put out a manifesto book, *En ny vänster* [A New Left] (Stockholm: Rabén & Sjögren 1966).

[5] Angus Deaton, *The Great Escape*, (Princeton: Princeton University Press, 2013), 82.

[6] James Riley, "The Timing and Pace of Health Transitions around the World," *Population and Development Review* 31, no. 4 (2005): 741–764, Appendix 1.

life chances in some parts of the world first meant increasing inequality. Global inequality of longevity began to decline after 1950, as measured by comparing the UK with Brazil, China, Egypt, and India.[7]

Existential inequality, for instance patriarchy and racism, is ancient. All major civilizations were patriarchal, although to varying extent. The Christian European least, and the Indic and the Sinic most misogynous. Patriarchy, like slavery, began to be questioned by the European Enlightenment, but survived the Atlantic Revolutions, except in Haiti. The nineteenth century was contrast-ridden. On the one hand, the slave trade was banned, and in the end slavery itself, and the second half of the century saw some extensions of women's rights, mainly in Northwestern Europe and the overseas European settlements. On the other hand, this was also the time of overseas settler large-scale violence against natives, of expansive European colonialism, and of its concomitant hardening of racist contempt and fear. The break came in 1945 with the discovery of Auschwitz and the defeat of its builders, which at least confined institutionalized racism to the US South and South Africa and opened up for a constitutionalization of de-patriarchalization.

By 1500 C.E., the world began to be regionally differentiated in per capita resources, while stark intra-societal inequality goes back to the Bronze Age, at least. By 1500, Western Europe was in the lead in terms of per capita income, an advantage which accelerated from the early nineteenth century, reaching more or less of a plateau after 1950, and slightly bending down in the current century.[8] Global inequality today is a manifestation of a world system centred on European-cum-North American advantage and power. It derives from three clusters of causal forces.

One is a global shift of technological and intellectual centre. Intellectual curiosity and technological edge, military and other, started to tilt towards Western-Central Europe in the fourteenth century.[9] By 1500, maritime Western Europe was prepared for world conquest.

Secondly, the European colonial conquests provided extraordinary sources of accumulation by American silver mining and plantation slavery, and by captive industrial markets, as in India. After the genocidal impact

---

[7] Göran Therborn (ed.), *Inequalities of the World*, (London: Verso, 2006), 21.

[8] Angus Maddison, *Contours of the World Economy, 1–2030 AD*, (Oxford: Oxford University Press, 2007), Table 2.1.

[9] William McNeill, *The Pursuit of Power*, (Oxford: Basil Blackwell, 1983), 98–113.

of the conquest, the Americas also contained an abundance of land and provided an escape from poverty to millions of Europeans. The rather minor Western European advance in 1500 made possible an enormous hoarding of global opportunities. With de-colonization and the independence of India and China, the world began to change after 1950, indicated by declining vital and existential inequality and a plateau of economic inequality with the re-start of economic growth in China and India.

A third reason of today's global inequality is the weakness of the popular classes of the Global South, in a broad sense, from independent business and the petite-bourgeoisie to peasants and workers. It is most clearly manifested in the phenomenon of the "informal economy," a largely rightsless area where almost ninety per cent of Indians have to find their living, in Latin America about half of all workers. The leaders of the victorious anti-colonial movements have tended to reproduce the duality of privilege and subalternity, and the enclaves of capitalism characteristic of colonial rule. Popular weakness also follows from the recent history and arbitrary boundaries of ex-colonial nations, easily divided by ethnicity, tribe, caste, religion.

5   What Are the Most Pressing Contemporary Challenges Concerning Global Inequality and How Do We Deal with Them?

The first pressing contemporary challenge concerning global inequality is the recent increase of privilege and power in the upper classes, a worldwide tendency towards a concentration of wealth and income among the very most advantaged. Particularly noteworthy is the widening gap between the upper and the middle classes. India is a telling example. In 2000, the top tenth of the population, on one side, and the middle and upper-middle classes (the middle forty percent), on the other side, had an equal share of the national income, meaning that the former had four times the average middle-class income. By 2015, the ratio was 7.8:1. Between the top 10 and the bottom 50 per cent the gap widened from 13:1 to 22:1.[10] This means a fortification of inequality, reinforced by the new political business of running democracies. Secondly, there is the issue, highlighted by the pandemic, of "informal" work, outside contracts and rights, about sixty per cent of the global workforce (ILO), a persistent scope of disempowerment despite poverty reduction. Thirdly, there is the enduring extreme poverty, of 690 million in 2021 (World Bank data). The 20th century longterm perspective of a transcendence of the socioeconomic system driven by private capital accumulation has not become less relevant in this century, when the inhabitableness of the planet is at stake, threatened by the lasting effects of ruthless accumulation. However, on shorter terms we should not forget that for all three of the issues mentioned there is a raft of known policy instruments, of progressive taxation, financial regulation, public ownership, infrastructure, and comprehensive services of education and health, universal rights to pensions and other social security, an enforcement of gender equality, equal and universal pre-schooling and schooling, universal legislation of labour rights, support of trade union organization, commitment to full employment including pro-employment growth strategies and, when and where needed, special employment programs, a targeting of extreme poverty abolition by cash transfers, education/training and employment provision. What is missing is sufficient egalitarian popular force, and therefore political will to tackle inequalities. On the contrary, after a virtually worldwide tendency towards less inequality in 1945–1980, the predominant trend after 1980 has been a reversal, to more inequality. The 21st century has started with large-scale egalitarian protest movements, alter-globalization movements, and regional movements in Latin America, the Arab world, and India in particular, but few of them have so far left enduring traces of lessening inequality. They do, however, indicate a potential of ending the socio-economic Counterreformation from the 1980s.

There is also for the first time an international Egalitarian Enlightenment of political economy, institutionalized in the UN special organizations, to some extent even entering into the World Bank and the IMF, and intellectually led by a phalanx of Nobel Laureates—Abijit Banerjee, Angus Deaton, Ester Duflo, Amartya Sen, Joseph Stiglitz—and other

---

[10] "World Inequality Database," accessed January 3, 2022, http://wid.world/data. For similar tendencies in the OECD, see Göran Therborn, *Inequality and the Labyrinths of Democracy*, (London: Verso, 2020), Table 4.

distinguished economists—Thomas Piketty and his collaborators at the Paris School of Economics, for instance—with some echo in small circles of enlightened bourgeoisie, e.g. the *Financial Times*, intellectually challenging existing inequalities.[11] It is not a challenge to the world system of unequal power. But the classical Enlightenment during the *anciens régimes* did inspire the Atlantic Revolutions.

[11] See e.g. The Editorial Board, "Virus lays bare the frailty of the social contract," *The Financial Times*, April 3, 2020. The article's subheading states: "Radical reforms are required to forge a society that will work for all.".

The Colonial Matrix of Power

Walter Mignolo

1 WHAT IS YOUR BACKGROUND AND HOW DID YOU BECOME INTERESTED IN GLOBAL INEQUALITY?

I sensed inequalities much before knowing what it was. I was born during World War II in Argentina's countryside, into a family of Italian immigrants. When I was seven years old, my parents moved to Corral de Bustos, a small town of 10,000 people located in the Province of Córdoba, so I could go to school. This town had been established by the nation-state on former indigenous lands. This was inequality at work. The state needed the lands to facilitate the establishment of British railroads in the country. Corral de Bustos was divided by the railroad into a wealthier, paved area in the south and a northern, poorer unpaved area in the north. People living in the south often said that in the north lived the "negros," who were not black, just brown-skinned. Some white people lived there too but the image was that by crossing the railroad, you entered into the "negros" zone. In the paved part of town, there were brown people too

W. Mignolo (✉)
Literature and Romance Studies, Duke University, Durham, NC, USA
e-mail: wmignolo@duke.edu

© The Author(s), under exclusive license to Springer Nature Switzerland AG 2023
C. O. Christiansen et al. (eds.), *Talking About Global Inequality*,
https://doi.org/10.1007/978-3-031-08042-5_5

but they were middle-class merchants or professionals and they were not seen as "negros."

My parents were poor, but of European descent, hence white-skinned. My father was a countryside laborer and when he moved to the town, he became a proletarian, working in a factory that produced agricultural machinery. At elementary and high school, my friends were the sons and daughters of middle-class and high-middle-class families. Their parents had nice houses compared to ours. Thus, in relation to the "negros" in the north, we were "better-off" but in relation to my middle-class friends, I felt "inferior." It was much later that I understood how race and class distinction and differential ranking (inequalities) molds our subjectivities without "knowing it" but certainly "sensing it." And that worked for both sides of the railroad: there is not outside of inequalities, everyone is involved in scales between privileges and destitutions.

2   What is Global Inequality?

Much later, I understood that what I sensed growing up as a teenager was the local manifestation of global inequalities. My first wake-up call was in the 1990s, when I became aware of "coloniality" and of the "colonial matrix of power (CMP)," two concepts that helped me to understand, rationally, what I already knew sensorially. Both concepts were introduced in the early 1990s by Peruvian sociologist, intellectual, and activist Anibal Quijano. Coloniality is the dark side of Western modernity.[1] Modernity promises salvation, progress, civilization, development, and democracy while it conceals coloniality, domination, exploitation, and expropriation. If you belong, or feel that you belong, to the sphere of modernity, you will most likely not sense coloniality. Coloniality is the will to power (the technique) hidden under the promises of modernity. The instrument of coloniality is the CMP (the technology). And the CMP is an abstract mechanism, like the unconscious in psychoanalysis. The CMP is in a nutshell the unconscious of Western civilization that discloses that double-bind of modernity/coloniality. The foundational assumption is that there is no modernity without coloniality, thus,

---

[1] Anibal Quijano, "Coloniality and Modernity/rationality," *Cultural Studies* 21, no. 2–3 (March 2007): 168–718; Walter D. Mignolo, "Delinking: The Rhetoric of Modernity, the Logic of Coloniality and the Grammar of Decoloniality," *Cultural Studies,* 21, no. 2–3 (March 2007): 449–514.

modernity/coloniality. Modernity is a rhetoric of salvation that conceals coloniality, the logic of exploitation, multiple oppressions, and expropriation. This theory is not well-known in Europe because, among other reasons, it was formulated in Spanish and in South America and is historically grounded in the colonial history dating back to the sixteenth century. What we see here is global power differentials and inequality in the area of knowledge. Economic exploitation and inequalities are legitimized by ways of knowing and knowledge persuading people that there is no economic horizon other than progress, development, and growth. That a person should look for happiness and that happiness consists of having more. Knowledge shapes people's senses and beliefs, until they realize how coloniality and the promises of modernity work.

Latin America during the Cold War was part of the Third World. Hence, unequal and dependent from the First and the Second Worlds. Therefore, it was unequal at the global economic and epistemic scale. Economically, it was underdeveloped, and epistemically, it was a space of culture, not knowledge, and of natural resources, not of ideas. Some of these main lines of global inequalities, I sensed at an early age in my small town. Consequently, decolonially speaking and derived from the analytics of coloniality, sensing and understanding inequalities depends on a) personal experiences and b) professional training that provides a rational explanation of personal experiences. Inequality is not a thing out there in the world but a relational structure of differential knowledge that creates material and psychological inequalities.

3   How Have the Places in Which You Have Lived and Worked Influenced Your View on Global Inequality?

Because my parents were poor, I quit high school and got a job as an office assistant in the factory where my father worked. Later on, in the early 1960s, I went to university in Córdoba city, the second largest in Argentina. I had to work to survive and pay for my studies and I got a job, first, at an insurance company and, later, in the public relations office at Kayser Industries. Finally, before moving to France, I worked in a Cinema Club for which I was a co-founder with other three guys that want to work for ourselves, not want to work for others. Some of my fellow students worked too, but most of them were supported by their parents. Public universities in Argentina at that time were totally free, so the expenses to live on were food, lodging, and entertainment. At university, we read and discussed the works of Karl Marx and Antonio Gramsci. These readings allowed me to become aware of class inequalities and understand my father's situation: he was a proletarian. I also understood that all my fellow students, except one, were from middle-class families. They understood theoretically what the proletarian class was but they had not experienced the life of a proletarian family.

It was much later, in the US and toward the end of the 1980s, that I understood racial and sexual inequalities. I also came to know that exploitation of labor in the Americas was built upon slavery, of indigenous and slaved African human beings. The Industrial Revolution ended slavery and replaced it by waged labor. In Europe, class obscured racism as the foundation of what is today called "capitalism." America did not exist for the inhabitants of the continent. It was a European name conveniently imposed by Europeans who controlled knowledge and naming. Inequality of knowledge is a component of racial inequalities: non-white "races" and non-Christian religions were destituted, first, by the growing hegemony of Christian theological knowledge and, later, by secular sciences of philosophy. In the sixteenth century, Moors and Jews were expelled from the Iberian Peninsula and their knowledge and beliefs were demonized. The advent of secular science and philosophy brought with it the notion of "primitives" and "barbarians" who were supposed to become "civilized." Civilization is a complex of knowing and praxes of living according to a standard that is supported by the actors who create their own standard and project it to universality.

4   WHAT ARE THE MAIN HISTORICAL CAUSES OF GLOBAL INEQUALITY?

Inequality is not a "thing" that can be treated as an entity, ontologically so to speak. Inequalities are relational. They are the outcome of inventing entities and entangling them in interlocked power relations. I call the logic of these relations "colonial differences." Colonial differences are not cultural differences. Cultural differences are visible, while power differentials are hidden. Pedagogically speaking, colonial differences are cultural differences entangled by power relations: there is a pole that produces inequalities and a diversity of planetary poles that endures them. That is how Eurocentrism works.

Let us tell two complementary stories in order to understand my concept of "colonial differences." One goes back to our ancestors thousands of years ago, when at some point hunting for food became killing to protect the herds—fenced and nurtured—that supplanted hunting. It was necessary to kill other animals who were competing for the same food in the flow and equilibrium of living on planet earth. The other story is shorter, it is only 500 years old, when a small group of Europeans from the Atlantic (from the Iberian Peninsula to the UK, going through France and the Netherlands), "discovered" not a new continent but a new way to possess and dispossess lands, exploit labors, and produce commodities for a global market made possible by the navigations across the Atlantic and the Pacific, which supplanted the role that the Indic and the Mediterranean Ocean had until the sixteenth century. Global coloniality, instrumentalized through the colonial matrix of power (CMP), is the cause of global disorders and inequalities, as I argued in an essay from 2015, "Global Coloniality and the World Disorder."[2]

CMP is a structure of control and management that operates in four domains. We can imagine each domain occupying a place in each of the four cardinal points. These four domains are: Knowledge and Understanding, Governance, Economy, and the idea of the Human or Humanity. Inequalities exist all over these domains. CMP is a machine producing injustice and inequalities and sold to the public as salvation, progress, civilization, democracy, and development. The pattern of inequalities in each domain has been established since the colonial revolution in the sixteenth century, which is transmitted in modern Euro-centered narratives as "discovery, conquest and colonization of America," and which destituted existing knowledge of the great civilizations of Tawantinsuyu (the territory of the Incas) and Anahuac (the territory of Aztecs and Maya), and of Turtle Island (the territory of the Iroquois and other First Nations in the North West, US and Canada). America did not exist, and something that does not exist cannot be discovered. It was invented.

---

[2] Mignolo, Walter. "Global Coloniality and the World Disorder. Decoloniality after Decolonization and Dewesternization after The Cold War," 2015.
  https://www.academia.edu/21395973/Global_Coloniality_and_the_World_Disorder_Decoloniality_after_Decolonization_and_Dewesternization_after_the_Cold_War (visited 19th December 2021).

After the revolutions of independence at the end of the eighteenth and mainly the first half of the nineteenth centuries, all the Americas—with the exception of Haiti—were managed by people of European descent. However, to paraphrase nineteenth-century Argentine intellectual Domingo Faustino Sarmiento, ideas are destituted but not killed.[3] Ideas die when they are no longer motivating or when the people embodying them are exterminated. Indigenous and African diasporic knowledge and praxis of living are well and alive in the insular and continental Caribbean. But there are also deadly ideas and, among them, the ideas that create inequalities in the name of progress, civilization, modernity, democracy, and development. Epistemic inequalities, inequalities of what is known and of the way of knowing exist today, and are visible in the privileges of the English language in Western sciences, the humanities, and mass media.

Epistemic inequalities legitimize the meaning of all other inequalities (political, economic, racial, and sexual) which are sustained on the belief that there are truths without parenthesis, that is, abstract universals.[4] That truth is something out there we human beings have to reach for and defend and whomever do not believe in the truth, I believe shall be either converted, marginalized, or, *in extremis*, eliminated. Global epistemic inequalities go hand in hand with global economic inequalities. Those who control money, also control meaning. Same for governance. The nation-state is a form of governance that grew "naturally" in the history of Western civilization but did not grow naturally out of any other co-existing civilization in the planet. However, the Western nation-state, complemented knowledge (political theory and political economy) with dispossession. Exploitation and multiple oppressions, contributed to create and maintain political inequalities globally. Last but not least, the Western concept of Humanity was also projected as a universal for the

---

[3] "Las ideas no se matan" [Ideas shall not be killed] is a well-known dictum in South America stated in the nineteenth century by Sarmiento, a main intellectual, activist, and president of Argentina between 1868 and 1874. See Evelyn Fishburn, "The Concept Of 'Civilization And Barbarism' In Sarmiento's 'Facundo'—A Reappraisal." *Ibero-Amerikanisches Archiv* 5, no. 4 (1979): 301–308.

[4] Trouillot, Michel-Rolph. "North Atlantic Universals: Analytical Fictions, 1492–1945." *South Atlantic Quarterly* 101, no. 4 (October 1, 2002): 839–858; Mignolo, W. D. "The Geopolitics of Knowledge and the Colonial Difference." *South Atlantic Quarterly* 101, no. 1 (January 1, 2002): 57–96.

human species while at the same time destituted a large portion of human-ness to privilege whiteness and heteronormativity. In sum, inequalities are all over because coloniality is all over. Those of us living on the planet have arrived to a point where the economy is the new religion and the core belief of most (if not all) people is that more is better, that happi-ness consists in possessing, succeeding to increase wealth and privileges. Thus, the myth of development that ultimately creates the conditions for competition and hate instead of cooperation and love.

5   What Are the Most Pressing Contemporary Challenges Concerning Global Inequality, and How Do We Deal with Them?

The most pressing contemporary challenge concerning global inequality is education. The priority of the current economy, known as capitalist, leads to the elimination of whatever does not produce wealth. There-fore, education (I do not mean schooling but education) and health are seen as encumbrance and unnecessary spending; or converted into business. Inequality is unavoidable in a capitalist economy and in a patri-archal culture crossed by racial differentiations (epistemic differentiations, not biological). By education, I do not mean institutions (elementary and secondary schools or universities), but conversations (organized, of course) about, and among people reflecting on why we do, what we do, why inequalities are maintained, why hatred is increasing, etc. Proceeding in this manner shifts the ways in which we (a general we) sense, feel, and think about what we do and why the conditions of inequalities were created and maintained. As Albert Einstein's well-known dictum goes, referring to physical theory, problems could not be solved with the same mindset that created the problems.

Hence if the mindset that created inequalities is global coloniality (the will to power, the technique) and the colonial matrix of power (the instru-ment, technology), inequalities cannot be addressed by focusing on the *content of inequalities* (economic, political, racism, sexism) but shall be addressed focusing on the *terms* (assumptions, beliefs, taken for granted), the rules of the game, that undergird and sustain the visible aspects of inequalities. This is the biggest challenge and it cannot be addressed by public policies. It requires a shift in people's senses, beliefs, thoughts, and knowledge and the way in which people relate to each other, including of course officers of the state, the corporations, and the finances.

To make this shift implies that inequalities cannot be properly addressed if it is assumed that inequality is something that is out there, independent of the actors, institutions, and languages that make and manage the socio-economic order built upon inequalities. *The world cannot be changed if the people who inhabit the world do not change.* Inequalities presuppose a scale that goes from people enjoying privileges (inter-state relations, white supremacy, heteronormative rightfulness, social opportunities to benefit from the privileges of the system) to people who are disfranchised, disqualified, and excluded. The main assumption to be addressed—the greatest of all challenges—is that which assumes that *the problem of inequalities is not that of the disfranchised, disqualified, and excluded but of the privileged.* Certainly, in a system created by global coloniality, the disfranchised and excluded *have problems,* but *they did not create inequalities.* Patriarchy *is not a women's problem,* although women *have problems* because of patriarchy. Patriarchy *is a male problem.* Blacks, First Nations, Muslims, people of color in general *did not create racial inequalities,* but *they have racial problems.* Racial inequalities have been created by Christian, white males and maintained by secular science and philosophy. Underdeveloped countries did not create inequalities. Inequalities were created by developed countries as they implemented the very idea of development. To reverse the way we, the people inhabiting the planet, feel, think, and believe, we must pay attention to education. The education needed requires a radical change of horizon where living on the planet is paramount, and harmony and equilibrium are the goals. Education is con-fused with schooling to preserve the idea that growth and development lead to happiness, while life on the planet continues deteriorating. And I do not think that technology can solve the problems that technology since the Industrial Revolution brought about. To do so, actors running governments, mass media, banks, corporations, Christianity (e.g., the privileged positions in global coloniality), have to give up some of their privileges and redress their assumptions and philosophies. That is hard. And that is the biggest challenge in the overcoming of inequalities today.

Colonial Logics and the Journey from the Third World to the First, and Back Again

Tung-Yi Kho

1 What Is Your Background and How Did You Become Interested in Global Inequality?

I was born and raised in Singapore when the language of the 'Three Worlds' was widely used to describe (material) realities around the world. In retrospect, such a conceptual framing of the world has had an impact on my understanding of it as a scholar, an activist, and a global citizen and would significantly contribute to my awareness of inequality on a global scale. Be that as it may, it is fair to say that my interest in global inequality was accidental, pressed upon my consciousness because of my peripatetic life circumstances beginning in the 1980s.

In the late 1970s and early 1980s, Singapore was considered a developing or Third World nation. Like almost all the nation-states that comprised the Third World, it was a young nation, having only gained formal political independence from the British in the early 1960s. Without

T.-Y. Kho (✉)
Centre of Cultural Research and Development, Lingnan University, Hong Kong, China
e-mail: kho.tungyi@yahoo.com

© The Author(s), under exclusive license to Springer Nature Switzerland AG 2023
C. O. Christiansen et al. (eds.), *Talking About Global Inequality*, https://doi.org/10.1007/978-3-031-08042-5_6

having to know exactly what they mean, the terms 'Third World' and 'First World' revealingly suggest that fundamental inequality exists in international relations and in the world order, with the former invoking a negative connotation vis-à-vis the latter. Given such concepts, one could not help but think that the First World served as an example for the Third World, the latter's eventual destination. The categories of such a scheme seemed to suggest the naturalness of the erstwhile global order of the 'Three Worlds' and the inevitability of progress within it. Singapore's leaders seemed to interpret its Third World designation in that vein, believing that 'progress' was predicated upon the country's graduation to First World status, which it did eventually in the 1990s, with a great sense of nationalistic pride.

Growing up in Singapore throughout the 1970s and 1980s allowed me to observe and experience the city state emerging out of relative impoverishment via 'modernization' and 'development' to become one of the world's most vital and prosperous nodes of the global capitalist economy. Perhaps because it had yet to be wealthy, the Singapore I grew up in was relatively equal with a rapidly expanding middle class, an increasing proportion of the adult population of which was engaged in wage-based, industrial employment. I say this as someone endowed with some socio-economic privilege. Coming from a relatively privileged middle-class background, with my father earning a good and secure income as a medical doctor, I was educated at a leading public school established by British missionaries—there were only public schools—and counted among my classmates the grandchildren of a few of the country's founding fathers. As it has turned out, a good primary school classmate happened to be the grandnephew of one of Asia's wealthiest men.

While a significant wealth gap would have existed between myself and the scions of the country's political and economic elites, the differences were never so outrageous to prompt me to reflect on inequality in Singapore. This attested to the relative equality of erstwhile Singapore society and to the nature of its economy at the time: a fledgling state-led industrial economy emerging from a low economic base with a quickly expanding middle-class population. This also affirms the idea that societies were much less unequal prior to 'modernization' and 'development'. The absence of drastic inequality between peoples of such different political economic standings, such as that extant between myself and my privileged classmates, would be unimaginable and impossible today. This was as much a function of the times—inequality was much less acute prior to 'development'—as the fact that today's Singapore has become a finance-oriented economy, in which wealth expands as a function of itself, often exponentially. Indeed, the latter is one of the chief mechanisms for perpetuating global inequality today.

In any case, it was Singapore's leaders' frequent and self-conscious declarations about the country's First World standing that led me to draw comparisons, first, with its neighbours in Southeast Asia and South Asia and then with the West whenever I was afforded the opportunities of travel. I began to understand that 'First World' was foremost an indicator of a country's material standing. I also noticed that the First World was constituted primarily by Western countries, notably, the United States, Western Europe, and countries in the Asia–Pacific such as Japan, and Australia. By virtue of what the World Bank called the East Asian Miracle, Singapore, along with the other East Asian tigers of South Korea, Hong Kong and Taiwan, were quickly ascending to the same league. Further questions emerged to challenge the dominant narrative: what gave rise to the First World on the one hand, and the Third World on the other? How does one move from the Third World to the First? As I discovered that the First and Third Worlds were materially coeval creations historically, it became apparent that inequality, on the level of the world-system, was a social creation systemically maintained through various policies over time.

2 What Is Global Inequality?

Global inequality refers to the global-scale disparities existing between individuals and groups in multiple, overlapping, domains: economic, intellectual, and in terms of access to opportunities. When speaking of global inequality, I am referring specifically to disparities pertaining to the material or economic realm. While inequality can be either due to innate (biological) factors or socially instituted circumstances, I will here only be dealing with inequalities that are the result of social contrivance and organization.

Owing to the global scale of the inequality being discussed, the typical unit of analysis is the nation-state. With 1% of the globe owning as much as 43.3% of the world's wealth, it is reasonable to say that global inequality is more pronounced now than it has ever been in human history (more about the reason for this below).[1] But while the best measure of global inequality we have are international comparisons, it is important to point out that national populations are not homogeneous but further stratified by racial, class, and gender divisions. This implies that inequality occurs not only between but within nations. The consequences of material inequality are, arguably, most urgent insofar as the economic dimension implicates the ability for the reproduction of one's life. In other words, the issue of equality in the material/economic domain is vital since it determines the possibility of physical sustenance, or not.

In the modern world-system, which exalts the economy to supersede all other dimensions of life, the money-production economy mediates much of the reproductive possibilities of biological as well as social life. As the money-production economy has expanded and encroached into more areas of life, especially the global commons, the attainment of food and shelter around the world today has become increasingly dependent on one's having access to money. This is a social construct, to be sure. Be that as it may, a lack of money can deprive one of life's necessities, even life itself, which compounds other types of inequalities. This again underscores the systemic, socially contrived nature of inequality at both local and global levels, the reason for why it continues to escalate today.

Essentially, my transnational life experiences have unambiguously revealed the nature of 'global inequality' today. The latter is constituted by egregious levels of material inequality—previously thought to be First World–Third World disparities—becoming a truly transnational and global phenomenon. We could reasonably speak of it as a pandemic of inequality, a universalization (or globalization) of First World–Third World inequalities across all societies. Accordingly, I understand 'global inequality' as a phenomenon of gaping material disparities not just existing *between* countries—as evoked by the anachronisms, 'First World' and 'Third World'—but, especially since the advent of the project of neoliberal globalization four decades ago, also extending into the 'rich' countries previously thought to constitute the 'First World'.

From a decolonial perspective, one could say that the colonial depredations formerly reserved for non-Western Others in the faraway lands of the Third World have been turned inwards, now also relentlessly devouring

---

[1] Credit Suisse Research Institute, Global Wealth Report, 2021. https://www.credit-suisse.com/about-us/en/reports-research/global-wealth-report.html (Visited 15 November 2021).

the populations of the former First World. It is only apt that we ask how things came to this. Indeed, what are the mechanisms that have led to the escalation of inequality on such a global scale?

3 How Have the Places in Which You Have Lived and Worked Influenced Your View on Global Inequality?

Since what we 'know' and how we 'see' are directly influenced by our social experiences, my views on global inequality have indelibly been shaped by my various experiences living, studying, and working in different parts of the globe, primarily, in Asia (Singapore, Hong Kong, China, Thailand) as well as in the West (Australia, the United States, and the United Kingdom).

I lived and travelled primarily in Asia in the 1970s and 1980s, between Asia and Australia in the late 1980s and 1990s, between Asia and Europe from the late 1990s until the early 2000s, in the US from 2006 to 2011, then between Asia (Hong Kong SAR, Mainland China, Thailand) and the UK ever since.

The privilege of travel and of dislocation offers an education like no other. The physical experience of being in different places allows one to empirically test and corroborate our familiar social concepts against the immediate reality. Dislocation compels us to suspend our conceptual certainties and subject them to the demands of evidence.

Hence, while the dominant concepts of the Three Worlds had prepared me to accept the sight of abject poverty in Bangladesh or Thailand in the 1980s, they were ill-suited for explaining the destitution and homelessness I witnessed in the US and UK in the 2000s and 2010s. What became increasingly obvious from my lived experiences was the paradox of witnessing 'First World' levels of affluence in the supposed Third World, and, conversely, 'Third World' levels of poverty in the supposed First.

4 What Are the Main Historical Causes of Global Inequality?

The material practices of colonialism as well as its logic (coloniality) have played a historic role contributing to the global inequality we observe today. I mean by 'colonialism' the phenomenon of more powerful polities subjugating and plundering weaker ones. Colonialism divided the world up into the haves and have-nots while the logic of 'coloniality' has sustained it. The logic of coloniality has ensured that the practices instituted by colonialism can continue despite formal decolonization, that is, the practices of colonialism can proceed without formal colonies.

It is owing to this historical fact about our modern world that decolonial scholars speak of modernity/coloniality as being coeval phenomena. To be sure, the world's truly First World War was colonial, beginning around the sixteenth century and lasting some four-plus centuries. Modernity/coloniality was gendered and racialized too, contingent on the masculinist domination of 'feminine' nature and women as well as the genocide of coloured indigenous populations; hence, the embeddedness of patriarchy and racism within modernity/coloniality. It was upon such a foundation of gender oppression and racist exploitation that the 'primitive accumulation' needed for the take-off of industrial capitalist development in the West could occur. Only then could modern 'society' be constructed along 'class' lines. Because of the global scale of their colonial projects, European and North American elites had conquered most of earth (84%) and controlled most of its population by the early twentieth century. The scale of this conquest ensured that modern European civilization would become the world's dominant civilization, furnishing the world with its dominant cultural references. The historical causes of global inequality are to be found here, even as many developments continue to be built upon this foundational re-ordering of the world by the West.

5   What Are the Most Pressing Contemporary Challenges Concerning Global Inequality, and How Do We Deal with Them?

The last forty years have witnessed coloniality predominantly taking the form of neoliberalism, a mode and model of global economic management propounded by Western political economic elites via the Washington Consensus, rendering the market the basis of all human and social relations. Neoliberalism entails two somewhat simultaneous movements/consequences: (i) marketization, and (ii) financialization. Because neoliberal ideology celebrates markets on the grounds that they have the ability to reflect real-time changes to market demand and supply via price-movements, the workings of financial markets have been considered to be the ideal expression of market forces. Yet, it is such fundamentalist market ideology and its practices of financialization around the globe that have caused inequality to reach the egregious levels seen today. As such, one of the consequences of neoliberal ideology has been the unrelenting corporate enclosure of what were erstwhile resource common via their marketization and financialization. These commons encompass resources vital for the production, reproduction, and functioning of life and society, which include the control of money and banking, land rights, food, health care, education, as well as natural resource rights. The protection of these commons to prevent their privatization remains most urgent in ameliorating global inequality.

As these erstwhile common public resources have been enclosed, they have become privatized and financialized 'assets' removed from the ambit of public regulation and provisioning. It follows that the 'financial gains' they now yield as assets are retained (expropriated) by private shareholders while the public is made to pay much more than what it costs to produce and supply them. Indeed, as the erstwhile commons are privatized and financialized, those private entities who control them are enriched while the public is compelled to pay more for services formerly provided at cost. Herein is the central mechanism of neoliberalism that has been responsible for the escalating levels of global inequality over the past four decades.

How do we arrest such a devolution towards escalating global inequality? It is important to note that one of the greatest problems posed by coloniality is the control it wields over knowledge, which is crucial for the perpetuation of the system. Indeed, even as global inequality has been increasing before us, one of the seemingly insurmountable challenges has been to find the conceptual vocabulary to articulate the injustice of the abovesaid processes. After all, the abovesaid neoliberal looting of the public commons is typically obfuscated by the invocation of the market as a symbol of individual freedom, democracy, and the like. In these quarters, financialization is legitimated as the just rewards for 'risk', even as they represent a blight to human and ecological well-being.

The way to grapple with this problem should be evident. There is an urgent and immediate need to break from neoliberal logics. Specifically, there needs to be the production of countervailing knowledge, an alternative conceptual vocabulary that responds to the ubiquitous but pernicious neoliberal dogma that all economic activities producing monetary value are 'valuable'. Neoliberalism wilfully confuses 'value' for 'the valuable' and thus dissolves the traditional distinction between 'productive' and 'unproductive' economic activity, a distinction which classical political economy made very clear. Such a conceptual erasure allows the value of financialization to be proclaimed on the basis of the 'monetary value' it creates, while dispensing with the need to ask whence such value comes. In other words, the dominant social discourse on financialization is steeped in coloniality: instead of denouncing financialization for exacerbating global inequality, it celebrates it for being 'valuable'. The consequence of accepting the notion of monetary value as the basis of 'value' is our seeming incapacity to launch any conceptually robust critique of financialization, thus allowing the looting of the public to proceed on the pretext that it is somehow societally beneficial.

Since the predominant mainstream (neoclassical) economic concepts of our time obscure these conclusions by conceiving of all monetary value as 'valuable' and all economic activities as 'productive', I would propose that we begin our pushback against the logic of neoliberal coloniality by reviving discussion of the distinctions between 'productive' and 'unproductive' economic activities as well as 'earned' and 'unearned' income. This is a critical discussion to be had across all sections of global society, at all venues claiming to play an educational function. Thankfully, one does not have to re-invent the wheel, for a discussion of such ideas had already begun in the nineteenth century as the central concern of classical political economy.

Restoring the conceptual vocabulary of classical political economy would offer us a clearer understanding of the parasitism that financialization entails. It would help us to immediately grasp the connection between neoliberal financial globalization and the dire levels of global inequality we witness today. Only when a critical mass sees, understands, and distinguishes between 'productive' economic activity and 'unproductive' rent-seeking activities—and denounces the latter—can we begin to deal with the problem of global inequality. Otherwise, the rentier class and their apologists will continue to have their 'free lunch' on us despite cynically claiming that 'there is no such thing as a free lunch'.

Unequal Entanglements: A Capitalist World System

Self-Interest and Similar Wealth Across Nations Equals World Peace

Branko Milanovic

1   What Is Your Background and How Did You Become Interested in Global Inequality?

The way I became interested in the topic of inequality was the product of two interests. The first was my interest in social issues which was reinforced when I learned about, or read, a few pieces of socialist literature in my high school years, such as Lenin's *Imperialism, the Highest Stage of Capitalism* and *The State and the Revolution*, works by Samir Amin and by Ernest Mandel, and Sartre's trilogy *The Roads to Freedom* (*Les chemins de la liberté*). The second was the fact that for the last two years of my undergraduate studies, I chose the area of statistics and operations research. Of obvious relevance to my interest in social issues became income distribution and the entire methodology of income distribution which I discovered at that time.

These two interests did not occur at the same time. My interest in social issues dates from my high school days in Brussels and was an outgrowth of my interest in international politics which I had almost since

B. Milanovic (✉)
City University of New York, New York City, NY, USA
e-mail: bmilanovic@gc.cuny.edu

I became aware of myself. There were big events in those days, many of them related to decolonization. Yugoslavia's policy of non-alignment also meant that my Belgrade elementary school teachers in geography and history often tended to speak of countries in Africa and Asia that were then gaining independence. It was done in part to magnify the importance of the then Yugoslav President Josip Broz Tito, but opened the eyes of many of us to the vast world around us. My family, and especially my grandmother who would always read political news in the morning (and who lived with us in a multi-generational household) was also an influence. I remember very vividly the big political crises of the time: the last stages of the war in Algeria (1954–1962), the murder of Lumumba in Congo (1961), the interminable war in Vietnam (1956–1975), the six-day war in the Middle East (1967), and the Soviet invasion of Czechoslovakia (1968). I talked about them with my family even when I was only twelve or thirteen years old.

Awareness of social issues, social classes, etc., developed later, when I was in high school in Belgium. This was in the late 1960s–early 1970s which, as everybody knows, was a tumultuous period much influenced by the events of 1968. Incidentally, I was also the witness of the 1968 student demonstrations in Belgrade against the "red bourgeoisie": a left-wing attack on the socialist regime where privileges and income differences were rife.

In my high school in Belgium, class distinctions between students were sharper than in Serbia. It was known whose parents were lawyers or doctors, and whose parents were middle-level clerks or workers. My first encounter with Marxist and left-wing literature happened in high school thanks to a couple of professors who were very knowledgeable and who themselves were very much on the left. They would often give up strict teaching (I remember that particularly well with our French literature professor) and we would engage into political or semi-political discussions. This was similar to what happened in my elementary school in Belgrade when professors would talk of decolonization. This later convinced me that students often learn more from professors who do not follow the syllabus than from those who do.

At the university studies in Belgrade in the mid-1970s, I chose to study, as I mentioned, the area of statistics. I always found statistics interesting, but its appeal was limited as long as I could not see its application to real-world problems. When I discovered income distributions, the Lorenz curve which displays the concentration of income among the wealthy, and other tools to study inequality the value of statistical knowledge suddenly became apparent.

It is important to point out that at the university, as part of the syllabus, we were not taught anything about income distribution. I "discovered" the area myself, by searching about it in books, in libraries and book-stores, and looking for some numbers. I remember how excited I was when I managed to find some French, and later some Yugoslav, data on wage and income distributions, and to compare them with the theoretical distributions.

The mid-1970s was also the time when hand-held calculators just became available. This was a huge advance that made calculations much easier. From today's perspective, this all seems extremely cumbersome. I still have notebooks with my drawings of the Lorenz curves using the quadratic regressions whose coefficients were calculated by "hand", that is by using the regression formulas and the hand-held calculator. It would not have been possible to do this just five years earlier. So, I benefited from the technological progress.

The work I just described on income distribution was something I did for myself. It was not part of any homework, there was nothing that was publishable. I did not even think in those terms: I knew nothing about economic publishing. It was just that I enjoyed calculating inequality indices, looking at distributions: it was a play, a thing with no goal external to itself.

My interest in *global* inequality came much later, in the mid-1990s when I was in the research department of the World Bank. I was in the unit where all the surveys that the World Bank either collects, or fields itself, would be brought together. Based on these surveys, the World Bank was, from the early 1990s, producing global poverty numbers using the famous $1 per capita per day absolute poverty line.

It very soon occurred to me that I could use the same data to "create" global income distribution. Back then, inequality was not considered a very important topic. Strictly speaking, there was even somewhat of a discouragement to work on inequality, particularly on Eastern European countries on which I was working then. It was believed by many people in the World Bank that those countries had low inequality anyway, and that we should not waste time studying it.

Thus, my interest in global inequality came from the realization that I could now calculate global income distribution, and that it was not done before because the data were not available. China did not have household surveys until 1984. The former Soviet republics had surveys, but the data were not released. Most African countries were unable to field surveys at regular intervals. The few studies of "global inequality" which existed covered up to two-thirds of the world population. By the mid-1980s, it was possible to do much more. And I was at the right place at the right time.

2   What Is Global Inequality?

For me, global inequality is simply inequality in income or wealth between all citizens of the world where in calculations each citizen is treated exactly the same. This implies that his or her income and wealth must be assessed using the same definitions, and equivalently across the world. It means adjusting for the differences in the real purchasing power between locations. This definition of global inequality is fairly technical and rather narrow. It looks at inequality between people considering only two variables, income, and wealth. But we can expand it to include education, life expectancy, access to water, electricity and other amenities, political and social freedoms. In all cases, the methodology is similar: we want to take a unit which is either an individual or a household and compare all such units across the world. Technically, it is not different from calculating national inequality. Politically, though global and national inequalities are entirely different, the difference stems from the fact that national inequalities are between individuals who share a government that does not exist at the global level where we do not have global government, nor any overarching global authority. Even our international organizations are precisely as the term says "international," that is, they are organization of nation-states, not institutions of world citizens.

3   How Have the Places in Which You Have Lived and Worked Influenced Your View on Global Inequality?

There is no doubt that having been exposed to different cultures and having lived in different countries is an extremely important element not only for the understanding of the issues of global inequality, but also for becoming a good social scientist. If you live your entire life in a very homogeneous environment, you can study things empirically as anybody else. However, the data work is enriched by our individual experiences: we can relate to the data that we collect or process much better if we know the country or the area. I thus find the American system of campuses, where students live in a bubble, a disaster for social sciences. Students are exposed to theories, but they never meet real people in subways. They become splendid econometricians, but if you ask them a simple sociological question about the individuals whose data they have manipulated, they are mum.

If you do not have political or historical knowledge of a certain country, you may not even be able to see certain data anomalies. We know that there are many issues stemming either from the negligence of the enumerators, mistakes in data entry, untruthful information, or even simple calculation errors. I have seen in several cases that people would miss some glaring mistakes or discrepancies because they would scarcely have any idea about the reasonable value for a given country or period. Now, the idea of what is a "reasonable" value comes from knowledge of history, readings, and thus a "bookish" type of experience, but it comes also from our immediate experience of having lived or visited some countries and thus from cultural familiarity.

As I mentioned before, having gone to school and lived in a socialist country like Yugoslavia was quite important in two ways: first, in my ability to know the socialist system, and in my exposure to the ideology of non-alignment. Belgium was also important: it was a richer country, more class-divided, and capitalist.

Having worked in the World Bank in Washington D.C. was useful not only because of the work I did there which would not have been possible anywhere else, but because the World Bank is the place that in terms of ethnic and racial diversity of people is probably unmatched (for a given surface area) anywhere in the world. But it is not a place where—despite working only one block from the White House—you would get much knowledge about the United States, however paradoxical it might seem. This is because the World Bank and the IMF have their own peculiar "globalistic" or even elitist cultures.

My knowledge of the US political and social scene improved much after I moved to the Carnegie Endowment for International Peace in 2003, a think-tank in Washington D.C. This was an entirely different world, much closer to the centers of US power, and directed toward influencing them.

I have also lived in England (where I have spent quite a lot of time over the years) and for almost two years in Spain (Madrid and Barcelona). Even the contrast between the last two cities, however small from the global point of view, was quite revealing especially as I was in Barcelona at one of the peaks of the Catalan pro-independence movement. The Spanish experience was also important as I learned Spanish and was able to better appreciate how lively the intellectual life in the Spanish-speaking world is.

My knowledge of Russian that I acquired first in elementary school in Yugoslavia and later in the World Bank by taking Russian lessons, and the fact that I was in Russia in the beginning of the process of transition, made me see the 1990s entirely differently from what was the dominant paradigm in the West. Obviously, the civil war in Yugoslavia, that lasted, with some interruptions, almost the entire decade, also contributed to my very different perception of transition to democracy and capitalism than what a person in New York or Warsaw (for very different reasons) might have. It also led me to reassess the entire question of identity, a question that is often left undiscussed in the context of the break-up of countries or empires.

By perhaps the luck of a draw (but also because I became very interested in Poland with the rise of Solidarity in 1980), I also spent quite a lot of time in Poland, working for the World Bank. I was in Poland before the transition while Poland was still under Martial Law (1981–1983), during the Round Table talks (March 1989), and then as the first non-Communist government after 1947 took power in August 1989.

But, as this list shows, my direct living experience was limited to Europe and North America. I have not lived, and that is of course a shortcoming, in Latin America, Asia, and Africa. I noticed in my own writings how important it is to have direct exposure to different parts of the world. My knowledge of Africa is not on a par with the rest of the world. The same may be true for some Asian countries. But I must single out, differently, China, about which I learned a lot in the 1960s and the 1970s during my very left-wing phase. It is also a country which I studied intensively in the past ten years, maintaining contacts with Chinese researchers. But I do regret that when I was younger, I never tried to learn Chinese.

4   What Are the Main Historical Causes of Global Inequality?

The historical causes of global inequality, taking "inequality" as I defined it in my answer to question two, are the Commercial Revolution and the Industrial Revolution which made Europe and later North America much richer than the rest of the world, technologically much more advanced, and militarily much stronger. These historical processes created income and power gaps between the two parts of the world. They also created what we call today "developing countries" or (slightly misleadingly) "emerging economies," and what until recently we called the Third World. Differences in wealth and power are the reason why European countries were able to colonize and control practically all the Americas, Australia, Asia, and Africa. At some point in the second half of the nineteenth century, inequality between countries and world citizens reached its peak.

The main causes of global inequality are thus differences in historical development. I did not want to put the emphasis on slavery and colonialism, because I see both as the *effects* of the large gap in wealth, income, and power. In other words, they would not have been possible had the gap in power not been so large.

5   What Are the Most Pressing Contemporary Challenges Concerning Global Inequality, and How Do We Deal with Them?

The most important global challenges are the pandemic (today), climate change (over the medium term), and reduction of global income and wealth inequality (over the longer term). The last point is a straightforward implication of what I already said in the answer to the previous question. For the peace to prevail—without which none of the issues can be solved—relative incomes and relative power of different parts of the world must become more equal.

This is something that Scottish Enlightenment philosopher Adam Smith saw: the huge disproportion in power between the West, and Africa and Asia led to the disastrous rule of the British East India company, colonialism, and wars. It "enabled them [Europeans] to commit with impunity every sort of injustice."[1] He thought that when different parts of the world are more balanced and deal with each other on a more equal footing, the very self-interest would dictate a more peaceful policy. Each side would be aware that an attempt to rule over the other might backfire, and that they might find themselves being under foreign rule. Consequently, "the equality of courage and force...by imposing mutual fear" would keep the world in peace.[2] Reduction of global inequality thus has a very strong element of peacebuilding in it. With huge differences in wealth and power, we cannot have durable peace. It is only when we are more or less equal, that our own self-interest would prompt us to be peaceful. To imitate one of the French physiocrats François Quesnay's maxims, I would say, "self-interest and similar wealth equals peace."

---

[1] Adam Smith, *The Wealth of Nations* (New York: Bantam Dell, 2003), p. 795.
[2] Ibid.

An Analysis Built on Global Measurement

James K. Galbraith

1   WHAT IS YOUR BACKGROUND AND HOW DID YOU BECOME INTERESTED IN GLOBAL INEQUALITY?

I am a professional economist, raised in the historical, institutional and political tradition of my father, trained formally at the University of Cambridge and at Yale in the 1970s, with an early career on the staff of the US Congress, ultimately serving as Executive Director of the Joint Economic Committee in the early 1980s. In that capacity, I organized one of the first modern-day hearings to inquire into rising inequality in the United States. Having moved to the University of Texas at Austin in 1985, I was drawn into the formal study of inequality in the early 1990s by a request from a foundation for a monograph on the then-burgeoning economic literature. I found that to make a useful contribution, it was necessary first to develop better *measures* of inequality than were then available. That work first surfaced in a book on the United States, *Created Unequal,* in 1998. By then, I had begun to attract a talented group of

J. K. Galbraith (✉)
Lyndon B. Johnson School of Public Affairs, The University of Texas at Austin, Austin, TX, USA
e-mail: galbraith@mail.utexas.edu

C. O. Christiansen et al. (eds.), *Talking About Global Inequality,*
https://doi.org/10.1007/978-3-031-08042-5_8

PhD students, including from Brazil, Portugal, China, Korea and Mexico as well as the US, and with backgrounds in physics, operations research, political science and budgeting. So we set out to extend our reach, in informal weekly research meetings that developed into the "University of Texas Inequality Project", now in its third decade. Our technique is based on measuring the inequality across *groups*—which may be geographic units such as provinces, states or counties, or industrial units such as standard industrial classification categories, or broader economic sectors. This approach has the great advantages of being very fast, very cheap, and very accurate as we have demonstrated in numerous studies. Eventually, we developed two major data sets that span almost the entire world for the years 1963 to 2014. One of them measures inequalities in industrial pay structures, based on data from the United Nations, while the other, the "Estimated Household Income Inequality" (EHII) data set, translates those measures in the familiar format of the Gini coefficient. These data sets, with over 4000 country-year observations for over 150 countries, are the largest of their kind that are consistent in the specific income concept that they measure, and that are calculated without filling gaps by averaging across years or between countries. They are widely used for applied research into movements of inequality over time, into comparative levels of inequality between countries, and into common patterns of change that affect the world economy as a whole.

2   What Is Global Inequality?

That is a complex question. There is no simple or single answer. Early researchers concentrated on the inequalities of income between rich and poor countries, using measures of average country income—a very primitive approach. Others modified that approach by weighting countries by their populations, which gives a very heavy weight to developments in China and India, with between them about 40% of the world's population. Others have tried to measure the inequality of incomes across persons or households, irrespective of nationality, in the world economy. And then there are attempts to measure differences and inequalities in wealth, a much more challenging and problematic task that we have not engaged with.[1] Our approach is to measure household income

---

[1] James K. Galbraith, "Sparse, Inconsistent and Unreliable: Tax Records and the World Inequality Report 2018", *Development and Change*, 50, no. 2 (2018): 329–346.

inequalities of a particular type—including in income government transfer payments (such as pensions) but not subtracting direct taxes (such as income taxes). We chose this concept because it can be estimated consistently for the largest number of countries and across the longest span of years, and therefore provides (in our view) the best basis for comparisons. Income is far from being a perfect measure! It is not a perfect synonym for well-being or happiness, and it does not perfectly predict health or life chances or freedom. Indeed, there are many aspects of the inequality of global economic life that mere income measures cannot capture. But in our view, there are advantages to sticking with something that can be defined and measured reliably, as this permits one to interrogate the data, to find common trends and consistent patterns, and so to understand the whys and hows of economic change. And it is reasonably clear that differences in income inequalities are associated with other kinds of inequalities as well, including inequalities of race and gender.

3   How Have the Places in Which You Have Lived and Worked Influenced Your View on Global Inequality?

I have lived in India as a child, in France and the UK as a student and I married into the People's Republic of China. I have traveled extensively in Europe including Russia, moderately in Latin America, some in China and not nearly enough in the rest of Asia or Africa. I served for four years, 1993–1997, as Chief Technical Adviser to the State Planning Commission of the People's Republic of China for Macroeconomic Reform, and I assisted the Ministry of Finance of the Hellenic Republic during the debt-and-austerity struggles of the early SYRIZA government in 2015. I maintain academic connections in Moscow, and I am the only American member, so far as I know, of the Free Economic Society of the Russian Federation, chartered by Catherine the Great in 1765. I am an elected member of the *Accademia Nazionale dei Lincei*, the Italian scientific academy established in 1604, and I have maintained extensive academic contacts in Italy in recent years. But most of my work on inequalities has been carried out in Texas, where my true exposure to the world has come from bringing students into the UTIP project. In addition to the countries mentioned above that were represented in the first cohort, students from Spain, Sudan, India, Iran, France, Belarus, Poland and Argentina

Fig. 1 An open-air market in Soweto, near Johannesburg, South Africa, one of the most unequal countries in the world; photograph taken by James Galbraith in October 2018

have made important contributions, and their perspectives have illuminated and enriched our work. I have also had the opportunity to present this work around the world on many occasions, including in South Africa, Korea, Germany, Italy, France, the UK, Argentina, Norway, Mexico, Brazil, Russia and China. A very wide group of international scholars and students have come into contact with our work over the years, and have helped me to improve my understanding of both general trends and particular cases and also anomalies and puzzles that have cropped up from time to time (Fig. 1).

4   What Are the Main Historical Causes of Global Inequality?

Current global inequalities are the historical by-product of conquest, imperialism, colonialism and dependency. They emerge out of the dynamics of capitalist expansion and the industrial revolution in the eighteenth and nineteenth centuries, out of the outcome of the Second World War and the end of the old European empires, out of socialist revolutions and their aftermath, and out of the financial hegemony of the United

States in the postwar world. Importantly, in our measures, the wea industrial countries in the 1960s, being possessed of a large working and middle class, were also much more egalitarian than the newly independent, agrarian and mining countries of the tropical zones. In the past forty years, movements of inequality as we have measured them are closely associated with changes in the global financial regime.[2] A first turning point occurred with the turmoil of the early 1970s, following which in many developing countries, inequalities declined with rapid growth and good export prices. A second, and more important global turning point occurred around 1981, with the rise of Reagan in the United States, Thatcher in Britain, the first postwar global debt crisis and the triumph of austerity and free-market economics, imposed through debt peonage. We observe a vast rise in inequalities around the world that begins in Latin America, Africa and parts of Asia. It continued in the early 1990s with the collapse of the socialist bloc and of the USSR, which generated chaotic increases in inequalities in Eastern Europe and the post-Soviet states. Then the pattern of rapidly rising inequalities moved to Asia, where liberalizations notably in India began in 1992, while those in Korea, Indonesia and Thailand culminated in the financial crisis of 1997. By our measures, the general level of income inequalities around the world now broadly resembles that of the tropical regions in the 1960s; only a handful of countries in Northern and Eastern Europe have preserved income inequality levels close to those of sixty years ago. However, since 2000, the pattern of increasing inequalities has been mixed, and broken by periods of improvement, notably in Latin America and in parts of Africa, where the neoliberal policies were eventually resisted and replaced, and also in Russia, which recovered (to a large degree) from the chaotic depression of the 1990s. In China, which was never a neoliberal economy and not (in recent times) subject to financial domination from abroad, the rise in inequalities of the early 1990s gave way to a broadening and deepening of prosperity, especially across provinces, that has reduced inequalities, somewhat, beginning in the middle 2000s.

---

[2] James K. Galbraith and Jaehee Choi, "Inequality Under Globalisation: State of Knowledge and Implications for Economics," *Real-World Economics Review*, 92 (2020): 84–102.

5   WHAT ARE THE MOST PRESSING CONTEMPORARY CHALLENGES CONCERNING GLOBAL INEQUALITY, AND HOW DO WE DEAL WITH THEM?

The topic of inequalities is fraught with myths; a key challenge lies in disabusing ourselves of mistakes and falsehoods. The broad movement of economic inequalities in the world is not due to mysterious forces of technology, it is not the product of developments in so-called "labor markets". It is not driven by the relative demand for and supply of an unmeasurable quantum called "skill". Still less is it the fault of migrant workers; it is not much influenced by trade, and it cannot be remedied by education, training or similar faux-policies that place the burden of action on the victims and not the perpetrators. In a world of financial capitalism, the supply of inequality is governed by the conduct and misconduct of finance, working through debt, interest burdens and speculations in international currency markets. Controlling the rapacity of global finance and its ideological circuit-riders, the neoliberal economists, is the most pressing challenge facing those who would like to get inequality in world incomes under control. Dealing with that challenge is, of course, a daunting proposition. Large countries like China, Russia, Iran, India should it so choose, and (to a degree) Brazil have the capacity to handle their internal affairs without reliance on external finance. With finance under control, they can then pursue programs of social development, affecting housing, health care, education, communications, water, power and other vital services for achieving what is known in some advanced development circles as "the good life" or "buon vivir". For smaller countries the problem is more difficult; the temptations of easy credit are great, and divide and rule has always been an effective tactic. Without the cooperation of the countries in the financial center—cooperation which is not to be expected—the smaller countries of the wider world need to band together, probably best on a regional basis, to create zones of global financial regulation and stability. Certain small countries have actually made progress in this direction at certain times in recent decades—Ecuador is an example, as are Bolivia, Uruguay and certain countries of East Africa. The challenge for them is to learn from effective examples, to expand the coverage of the successful cases, and ward off the predatory attentions of false friends and ideologues. The challenge for those in the rich countries who care about this issue is to try to get our own financial sectors under effective regulation and control, and to support progressive forces where and as they emerge in the developing regions.

How the Global Movement of Money and People Turns the World Upside Down

Alastair Greig

1   WHAT IS YOUR BACKGROUND AND HOW DID YOU BECOME INTERESTED IN GLOBAL INEQUALITY?

My earliest intellectual passion, throughout the 1980s, was development studies, in particular the efforts of various revolutionary regimes (from the Russian Revolution 1917 through to the Nicaraguan Sandinista Revolution 1979) to achieve radical social change within the constraints of the world capitalist system. I was also politically active during this period in the Australia-wide solidarity movement that opposed US interference in Central American affairs, and through this movement, I spent six months during 1985–1986 helping to construct a primary school in Masaya, Nicaragua.

I then became a postdoctoral fellow exploring technological change within the Australian clothing industry, a project which initially sounded depressingly parochial to me. Yet, ironically, this project became the catalyst that raised my awareness of the 'global' dimensions of inequality. Australian industry was experiencing a sharp reduction in tariff protection,

A. Greig (✉)
Australian National University, Canberra, ACT, Australia
e-mail: Alastair.Greig@anu.edu.au

and many clothing firms relocated their labor-intensive sewing operations to lower-cost countries, such as Fiji, China, and Cambodia.

However, other clothing firms dependent on rapid market changes took advantage of the depressed labor market to establish complex local subcontracting chains that relied on exploiting 'outworkers' under flexible irregular contracts. By 1990, these outworkers were typically more recent migrant women from Vietnam who worked from home and were paid piecework for sewing bundles of clothing panels delivered to them by sub-contractors.[1] For this vulnerable section of the workforce, the globalization of the clothing industry was a process in which they experienced higher levels of exploitation, poorer working conditions, and loss of entitlements. Principal retailers and manufacturers often denied any responsibility for outworker exploitation, but my project showed that this denial could not be sustained in the light of the 'quality assurance' procedures powerful companies promoted along their lengthening local and global chains of production.

The experience of the restructuring of the Australian clothing industry alerted me to the multifaceted nature of contemporary global inequality, along the lines of class, gender, and ethnicity. I became aware of how the costs and benefits of this process were unevenly distributed, and how this exacerbated inequalities on a truly global scale.

2   What Is Global Inequality?

Due to the dramatic social, economic, and technological changes that have occurred over the past few decades, the operative word in this question is the adjective 'global' rather than the noun 'inequality'. When I began my academic career in Australia during the 1980s, this question would have provoked a discussion on the differences in wealth and income between different countries, especially between the 'first world' and the 'third world'. These inequalities also manifested themselves in unequal power relations between nation-states. Indeed, during the 1980s, my political activism and my PhD in sociology dealt with the unequal power relations between the USA and Nicaragua.

Today, 'global inequality' evokes a more complex network of social, economic, and technological relations. My example of the Australian

---

[1] Alastair Greig, "Sub-Contracting and the Future of the Australian Clothing Industry," *Journal of Australian Political Economy*, 29 (May 1992): 40–62.

clothing industry illustrates this transformation. It involved the dismantling of post-World War II nationally centered regulatory compromises between the states, organized labor and capital, and its replacement from the 1980s onwards with a more deregulated market environment, where the decisions of all actors within nation-states are conditioned by multiple extra-territorial relations. These range from the differential costs of labor across the world, technological change, bilateral and multilateral trade agreements, including 'competition policies'.[2]

This regulatory shift has strengthened the hand of capital and weakened that of organized labor. Consequently, throughout the world, the conditions of labor have deteriorated, leading to growing levels of inequalities between the rich and poor within nation-states. Everyone experiences this era as an 'age of uncertainty', but there are contrary impacts depending on a person's social status. It increases the power and wealth of the richest while putting downward pressure on the wages, conditions and security of the rest of the population.[3]

3   How Have the Places in Which You Have Lived and Worked Influenced Your View on Global Inequality?

I share with many Australians the experience of immigration, and both my place of birth and my destination in Australia have shaped my views on global inequality.

I was brought up in Glasgow, Scotland and in my youth lived for its football culture. However, my father saw a city in decline, and he faced an uncertain future in the shrinking Clydeside shipbuilding industry. As my parents' standard of living deteriorated, in 1976 they decided to move the family to Australia. So, by the age of 15, I had already sensed that social transformation was an ambivalent, apprehensive, and somewhat foreboding process that could rip people from the comfort of their hearth, even if others spoke of this process as modernization and a radiant future.

---

[2] David Peetz, *The Realities and Futures of Work* (Canberra: ANU Press, 2019).

[3] William Tabb, *Economic Governance in the Age of Globalization* (New York: Colombia University Press, 2004).

A decade later, settled in Australia, I read Julienne Schultz's *Steel City Blues*, which described a similar experience among steel workers in Wollongong, Australia. Schultz argued that 'restructuring' was a euphemism that hid the intertwined phenomena of corporate growth and job loss.[4] As I mentioned earlier, it was while analyzing the clothing industry in the early 1990s that I started to appreciate the global nature of these unequal outcomes, part of what the Austrian economist Josef Schumpeter called 'creative destruction'.[5]

Even though evidence shows that the gap between the richest and poorest in Australia is wider now than it was thirty years ago, and despite the alarming rise in the number of people who eke out a precarious existence, Australia remains a country with a strong ethos of egalitarianism.[6] In the same way that the euphemism of restructuring can mask unequal outcomes, the rhetoric of egalitarianism can blunt the political reactions to widening inequalities (Fig. 1). Living in Australia underlines the value of studying inequalities from multiple perspectives: from objective and statistical analyses of trends and processes (realism) to more subjective approaches that document individuals' experiences of inequality and how they frame it (interpretivism).[7]

4   What Are the Main Historical Causes of Global Inequality?

I find it helpful to approach this question using a theoretical orientation that establishes a continuity between earlier stages of global inequality with our contemporary phase.

[4] Julienne Schultz, *Steel City Blues* (Melbourne: Penguin Books, 1986).

[5] Joseph Schumpeter, *Capitalism, Socialism and Democracy* (New York: Harper Books, 1975).

[6] Peter Davidson, Bruce Bradbury, Melissa Wong and Trish Hill, *Inequality in Australia, Part 1: Overview* (Sydney: Australian Council of Social Service and UNSW, 2020) http://povertyandinequality.acoss.org.au/wp-content/uploads/2020/09/Inequality-in-Australia-2020-Part-1_supplement_FINAL.pdf (accessed January 3, 2022); Tanya Carney, and Jim Stanford, *The Dimensions of Insecure Work: A Factbook* (Canberra: The Australia Institute, 2018) https://www.tai.org.au/sites/default/files/Insecure_Work_Factbook.pdf (accessed January 3, 2022).

[7] For a realist perspective, see Frank Stilwell, *The Political Economy of Inequality* (Cambridge: Polity Press, 2019); for an interpretivist perspective see Mark Peel, *The Lower Rung* (Cambridge: Cambridge University Press, 2003).

Fig. 1 Epicormal buds emerge on eucalyptus trees in Murramarang National Park after the devastating south-eastern Australian bushfires of 2020. The pressing challenge of global inequality will have to involve enhancing our collective environmental security and working towards environmental justice; Photograph by Alastair Greig's partner, Sallyann Ducker

These origins of global inequality can be traced to the mercantile plunder associated with European colonial expansion from the end of the fifteenth century onwards. This underwrote the primitive capitalist accumulation that led to European banking and later industrial capitalism, along with the proletarianization of the European workforce. Immanuel Wallerstein and Arghiri Emmanuel among others labeled this global form of inequality 'unequal exchange', whereby the economies of the colonized societies were subordinated to the needs of capital accumulation centered in the most powerful regions of the world economy.[8]

This unequal exchange survived the twentieth century, despite the end of formal colonialism, as the USA assumed the prime position as global hegemon. The world capitalist system metamorphosed again during the

[8] Immanuel Wallerstein, *World-Systems Analysis* (Durham NV: Duke University Press, 2004); Arghiri Emmanuel, *Unequal Exchange: A Study of the Imperialism of Trade* (New York: Modern Reader, 1972).

last decades of the twentieth century, as capital took advantage of more deregulated financial markets and the revolution in communication and distribution networks. In this new global phase of inequality, capital was afforded opportunities for greater mobility, while nationally based labor forces competed with each other in a downward spiral of deteriorating wages and conditions. Labor and capital remain intertwined in a global web of compounding inequalities.

When I began studying the restructuring of the Australian clothing industry in the early 1990s, I found that the explanations associated with 'the new international division of labor', 'post Fordism', and 'disorganized capitalism', were consistent with the historical model outlined by Wallerstein, if we consider our epoch as the latest stage of the world capitalist system.[9] The most striking feature of this epoch has been that while the world has never been so interconnected, the rich and the poor even within the same city experience different lifeworlds. To paraphrase Robert Reich, no longer do they rise and fall in the same national boat in the shifting tides of the global economy; it is now every person for themselves.[10] Global inequality has contributed to a fracturing of our sense of community and social solidarity.

5   WHAT ARE THE MOST PRESSING CONTEMPORARY CHALLENGES CONCERNING GLOBAL INEQUALITY, AND HOW DO WE DEAL WITH THEM?

There are two types of challenges that need to be confronted when tackling global inequality; first tackling the trends outlined above; and secondly, challenging deeper existential threats.

With respect to the first set of challenges, reversing the trend towards global inequalities requires a multilevel (from the local to the global regulation) and a multidimensional approach (including class, gender, ethnicity, among other dimensions). The best means of effecting progressive change involves listening to those most affected by inequality. In

---

[9] Folker Fröebel, Jürgen Heinrichs and Otto Kreye, *The New International Division of Labour: Structural Unemployment in Industrialised Countries and Industrialisation in Developing Countries* (Paris: Éditions de la Maison des sciences de l'homme, 1980); Alain Lipietz, *Miracles and Mirages: The Crisis of Global Fordism* (London: Verso Press, 1987); Scott Lash and John Urry, *Disorganized Capitalism* (Cambridge: Polity Press, 1988).

[10] Robert Reich, *The Work of Nations* (New York: Vintage Press, 1992).

Australia, an important starting point in this regard would involve supporting the 2017 Uluru Statement from the Heart which proposes giving greater voice in Federal Parliament to the nation's most disadvantaged group, Indigenous Australians.[11] At a global level, reforms could include tighter regulation of international financial transactions, greater transparency with respect to corporate-state contracts, enforcing international labor standards, and a moratorium on—or canceling of—the debt of poorer nations. At a national and sub-national level, reforms include more progressive taxation, guaranteed basic income, affordable housing, universal health care, democratic budgeting, and democratic nationalization.

Approaches based on individuals (or nations) 'catching up' with the wealthy have proven to be illusory and are now beyond the planet's ecological threshold. In the future, a redistributive logic based on meeting social needs and ecological protection must override a growth logic based on individual consumption. Reforms must involve enhancing our collective environmental security and working towards environmental justice.

If current trends towards global inequality continue, I have no doubt that the wealthy will use their power to protect themselves from the global environmental catastrophe that they themselves have promoted, leaving the rest to the world's population to face the consequences of an apocalyptic future. Fundamentally, challenging global inequality is the most effective means of challenging our current climate emergency.

---

[11] "From The Heart," https://fromtheheart.com.au (accessed January 3, 2022).

The Need to Centre Imperialism

Ingrid Harvold Kvangraven

1   What Is Your Background and How Did You Become Interested in Global Inequality?

I grew up partly in a small village in rural Norway and partly in the capitals of Botswana, Mozambique and Cambodia, as the child of a teacher and a city council employee turned aid worker. The immense inequality I was faced with at a very early age, both between countries and within them was instrumental in shaping my interests and outlook on life later. When my mom told me that I had malaria in Maputo (Mozambique) at the age of 7, I dramatically and naively saw my life flashing before my eyes as I thought I was going to die, having read it was the disease most people died from in Africa at the time. I found it difficult to grasp when my mom then explained to me that the fact that a disease kills a lot of people does not mean that it's not easily treatable and that I wouldn't die because I had access to a good hospital. That was an overwhelming understanding about a system that let the rich live and the poor die, laying bare my own privilege and immense global injustice. Being faced with inequalities

I. H. Kvangraven (✉)
King's College, London, UK
e-mail: ingrid.kvangraven@kcl.ac.uk

C. O. Christiansen et al. (eds.), *Talking About Global Inequality*,
https://doi.org/10.1007/978-3-031-08042-5_10

and injustices like this throughout my childhood and adolescent years, I developed a strong interest in trying to understand how they came about and how to counter them.

I therefore went on to pursue undergraduate and master's degrees in interdisciplinary development studies programmes at the University of Oslo and the London School of Economics and Political Science, always focusing on the unequal economic systems and the often-inadequate attempts to address these inequalities (e.g. through microfinance or IMF programmes). I took courses across different fields, but somehow always found Economics to be the least satisfactory, even though my research interests were very much economics-oriented. I was very excited to discover heterodox economics towards the end of my master's programme, which ultimately led me to pursue a PhD at The New School in New York City. Unlike the mainstream economics courses, I had taken, I was thrilled to find an approach to economics that took the role of power relations in determining economic relationships as a starting point, which is essential to even begin to explain the massive global inequalities we see in the world. Under the supervision of Sanjay Reddy at The New School, I had the freedom and opportunity to explore global inequalities along different lines during my PhD, including through exploring dependency theory as an intellectual project, inequalities pertaining to how African countries are integrated into the global financial system, and the inadequacies of localized approaches to poverty that do not challenge the broader constraints to development, like financial inclusion.[1]

2   WHAT IS GLOBAL INEQUALITY?

Global inequality is the unequal distribution of resources and opportunity across the world. You can evaluate it across different yet interrelated axes, such as health and educational outcomes, economic outcomes and possibilities for self-determination, but also across different groups, for

[1] Aleksandr V. Gevorkyan and Ingrid Harvold Kvangraven, "Assessing Recent Determinants of Borrowing Costs in Sub-Saharan Africa," *Review of Development Economics*, 20, no. 4 (2016): 721–738.

Paulo Dos Santos and Ingrid Harvold Kvangraven, "Better than Cash, But Beware the Costs: Electronic Payments Systems and Financial Inclusion in Developing Economies," *Development and Change*, 48, no. 2 (2017): 205–227.

example between countries, individuals, gender, class and race. The study of "global inequality" thus becomes a vast and complex field.

In my own work, I've focused mostly on inequality between countries. If we think back again to the Norwegian 7-year-old girl in Maputo, the differences between her and a Mozambican child living in poverty are of course complex and cut across many identities, including race and class. But it seemed to me at the time that the overwhelming difference was nationality, especially given the environment I came from in rural Norway where my friends from less advantaged backgrounds still had access to health, education, shelter and relatively good material lives. According to economist Branko Milanovic's empirical work, unskilled workers' wages in rich and poor countries often differ by a factor of 10 to 1, and more than 80% of global income difference is due to the large gaps in mean incomes between countries.[2] This observation supports the emphasis on geography which underlies a lot of dependency theory work. I don't mean to say that this is the only form of inequality that matters—inequalities in race, class and gender are essential to understand the complexities of global inequalities and barriers to equal outcomes—but it is a form of inequality that is important to unpack and challenge.

3 How Have the Places in Which You Have Lived and Worked Influenced Your View on Global Inequality?

I appreciate this question because it forces us to consider how our own background and positionality affects one's understanding of the world. This is important in an environment where academics very often present themselves as providing objective and neutral research although our viewpoints and perspectives are always shaped by our experiences. Theoretical and empirical approaches in academia are also always shaped by worldviews and ideologies.

My own background did not only make me acutely aware of the massive inequalities that exist in the world, but also provided a foundation for me to seek its systemic nature. Although we as children and teenagers would always learn about the national histories and politics of

---

[2] Branko Milanovic, "Global Inequality: From Class to Location, from Proletarians to Migrants," *Global Policy*, 3, no. 2 (2012): 125–134.

the countries in which we lived, contrasting the situation in Mozambique and Cambodia on the one hand (very different countries economically, historically, politically, and culturally) and Norway on the other, left me feeling that highly localized explanations were incomplete. While studying development studies at the University of Oslo I was looking for volunteer opportunities, and therefore quickly gravitated away from most NGOs which were concerned with aid projects, towards the others which addressed global inequalities from a global and systemic standpoint. That led me to volunteering for Debt Justice Norway and eventually working for them full time from 2011 to 2013, between my master's and my PhD.

In short, my early meeting with global inequality encouraged me to engage with organizations and research that invoked global inequality as a starting point. As a teenager in the early 2000s, this meant subscribing to material from the socialist youth party in Norway, which was the only youth party I found that had addressing inequality as a central priority at the time. Later, it led me to Debt Justice Norway, and finally to the discovery of heterodox economics and dependency theory which is a central area of my work and research.

4   What Are the Main Historical Causes of Global Inequality?

Global inequality can be understood with different axes and lenses, depending on the question one is posing. For instance, to understand race and gender-based inequalities, the necessity to trace the historical origins of patriarchy, white supremacy, colonialism, the slave trade and Eurocentrism. If one is interested in class-based differences and inequalities, it is important to understand the development of capitalism and intersectionality of class with other forms of structural inequalities. If we are interested in inter-national inequalities, then development of capitalism and the colonial period is key. As argued in my work on dependency theory, a global historical approach to global inequality is important tracing the role of colonialism in shaping economic relationships and structures in particular ways that remain durable.[3] For example, the way capitalism

---

[3] Ingrid Harvold Kvangraven, "Beyond the Stereotype: Restating the Relevance of the Dependency Research Programme," *Development and Change*, 52, no. 1 (2021): 76–112.

developed in South Korea laid the foundations for a very different kind of economy than the way it developed in African colonies.

In my recent research with political scientist Kai Koddenbrock and development economist Ndongo Samba Sylla, we found that the ways in which economic and financial systems were structured in Senegal and Ghana during the Colonial period, was primarily to the benefit of British and French capital. This led to the divorce between finance and real domestic production, which to a large extent has prevailed since independence.[4] In both Senegal and Ghana, the colonial banking system was set up with the primary aim to ensure that the monetary system worked smoothly and settled the accounts of the colonial economy, rather than increasing the volume of money or to finance structural change domestically. Indeed, in both countries, the bank's primary task was to protect and preserve the interests of the colonial trading companies from indigenous competition. In other words, it ensured a divorce between the financial system and domestic production. In fact, banks in Ghana were prohibited from lending to West African smallholders because of colonial laws not recognizing African private property in land. Given these insights, it is important to include historical analyses in work on global inequality, especially as it is to a large extent neglected in economics (as we found in a recent survey).[5]

5   What Are the Most Pressing Contemporary Challenges Concerning Global Inequality, and How Do We Deal with Them?

In 2020, I wrote for Open Democracy, "If we want to tackle global inequality, we need better economic theories".[6] The key argument is that despite increasing global inequality, economic theory has been inadequate

---

[4] Kai Koddenbrock, Ingrid Harvold Kvangraven and Ndongo Samba Sylla, "Beyond financialisation: the longue durée of finance and production in the Global South." *Cambridge Journal of Economics* (2022). https://doi.org/10.1093/cje/beac029.

[5] Ingrid Harvold Kvangraven and Surbhi Kesar, "Why Do Economists Have Trouble Understanding Racialized Inequalities?" *Institute for New Economic Thinking*, 3 August, 2020. https://www.ineteconomics.org/perspectives/blog/why-do-economists-have-trouble-understanding-racialized-inequalities (accessed January 3, 2022).

[6] Ingrid Harvold Kvangraven, "If We Want to Tackle Global Inequality, We Need Better Economic Theories." *Open Democracy* 11 June 2020,

in analysing the historical and political origins of economic inequality over the past few decades. The first step towards understanding global inequality is therefore to centre our analysis on theories that take global inequality as a starting point. For economists, it is particularly important to pay attention not only to economic income inequality between countries and individuals, but also engage and focus on various structural inequalities that plays out across gender, race and class.

Beyond the need for better theorizing about global inequality, there are key policy issues that are urgent and have become even more so in wake of COVID-19. One key issue is mounting debt, as the pandemic led to dramatic reversals of capital flows, indeed the largest outflow ever recorded.[7] Many developing countries have experienced currency depreciations as well as severe debt and liquidity problems. As the much-needed fiscal space of developing countries is constrained by these external factors, there are some key policies that have been put forwards by activists, such as debt moratoria, emergency loans and debt relief. IMF and the World Bank responses have been wildly inadequate so far, and in many cases, they are attaching harmful conditionalities to the emergency loans to developing countries.[8]

Short-term policies and fixes are urgent and important, but in the longer term it's essential to take a more structural approach to these inequalities that COVID-19 has laid bare. Given that debt is often a symptom of deeper problems, we need to challenge the very roots of the system that allows these debt crises to recur in the first place. To do so, it's

https://www.opendemocracy.net/en/oureconomy/if-we-want-tackle-global-inequality-we-need-better-economic-theories/ (accessed January 3, 2022).

[7] The International Monetary Fund, "The Great Lockdown: Worst Economic Downturn Since the Great Depression." *IMF Press Release,* March 23, 2020, https://www.imf.org/en/News/Articles/2020/03/23/pr2098-imf-managing-director-statement-following-a-g20-ministerial-call-on-the-coronavirus-emergency (accessed January 3, 2022). and S. Razavi, H. Schwarzer F. Durán Valverde, I. Ortiz and D. Dutt. "Social policy advice to countries from the International Monetary Fund during the COVID-19 crisis: Continuity and change." ILO Working paper 42. https://www.ilo.org/global/publications/working-papers/WCMS_831490/lang--en/index.htm (accessed September 5, 2022).

[8] Allison Corkery, Andrés Chiriboga-Tejada, Adrian Falco et al., "Austerity Is Killing Ecuador. The IMF Must Help end this Disaster," *The Guardian,* 29 August, 2020, https://www.theguardian.com/commentisfree/2020/aug/29/ecuador-austerity-imf-disaster (accessed January 3, 2022).

important to address the way capitalism generates uneven development—both inherently as a system and at the global level when interacting with institutions shaped by colonialism, structural inequalities across different groups, as well as how imperialism itself plays out in our contemporary global system, sustaining global inequality.

The Crisis of Neoliberal Capitalism

Gilbert Achcar

1 WHAT IS YOUR BACKGROUND AND HOW DID YOU BECOME INTERESTED IN GLOBAL INEQUALITY?

I was born in French-ruled Senegal, which I left at the age of eight in the year it became independent (1960). Both my schooling in a mixed multi-coloured environment and the belonging of my parents to an ethnic category—the Lebanese—which was itself an object of racial contempt from citizens of the French colonial power, created in me an early sensitivity to inequality and injustice.

Later on, during my teenage years in Lebanon, this sense took a Christian twist: I became active in the Young Christian Students (Jeunesse étudiante chrétienne, JEC), an international youth movement linked to the Catholic Church. During the 1960s, this movement shifted politically to the left in the context of the global left-wing youth radicalisation that characterised this historical period. My next step, like many of my generation who had been through the JEC, was to become plainly Marxist. That was partly in response to the revulsion against the war waged by

G. Achcar (✉)
Development Studies, SOAS University of London, London, UK
e-mail: ga3@soas.ac.uk

the United States in Vietnam, compounded soon after by the shock of the 1967 Arab–Israeli war and the new round of tragedy incurred by the Palestinian people.

These experiences and ideological evolutions constitute the background of my interest in inequality at all levels, local as well as global and social as well as horizontal. My political interest in global inequality translated into a scholarly interest in development studies and imperialism. In 1974, I started a doctoral thesis on Egypt's experience in development, which I had to abandon due to the war in my country. I resumed my doctoral studies in Paris in 1990, with a thesis on US imperial strategy written on the backdrop of the first Washington-led war on Iraq in 1991.

When I was offered a chair at SOAS, University of London, in 2007, the purpose of my recruitment was that I set up and convene an MSc programme on Globalisation and Development. This was the final stage in the personal and intellectual trajectory that led me to develop a special interest in global inequality.

2   What Is Global Inequality?

There is no singular global inequality, of course: there are many global inequalities. Most people tend to think of global inequality as referring to the inequality between countries and world regions. The initial surge of global interest in this type of inequality occurred in the 1970s. It is in 1974 that the United Nations' General Assembly adopted its famous resolution calling for a "New International Economic Order based on equity, sovereign equality, interdependence, common interest and cooperation among all States".[1]

The dominant perception of global inequality is still primarily about the global fracture between the Global North and the Global South, i.e. between, on the one hand, North America, the European countries including Russia, Japan and South Korea, with the addition of Australasia, and on the other hand the rest of the world. But this geo-economic perception is inaccurate. For, if the chosen criterion is GDP per capita, Russia would be closer to the poorer category than to the richer, let alone

---

[1] UNGA, "Declaration on the Establishment of a New International Economic Order" (New York: Resolution adopted by the General Assembly, 3201 S-VI, 1974), http://www.un-documents.net/s6r3201.htm.

the fact that the rich hydrocarbon monarchies of the Gulf Coc
Council belong to the upper tier.[2]

The global inequality that I am most interested in cuts acrc
tries and world regions: it is the social inequality between tl_
rich and the world poor, both categories existing in all countries and
nations. The attention paid to this specific type of global inequality
increased tremendously in the neoliberal age starting from the 1980s. It
was highlighted by a powerful symbol: the "champagne glass" image of
global economic disparities, first produced by the United Nations Development Programme in its 1992 *Human Development Report*.[3] Based
on economic distribution within countries, the report assessed socioeconomic inequality among the global population taken as a whole, finding a
ratio of 140 to 1 of per capita income between the richest quintile of the
world population and the poorest quintile. This inequality has immensely
worsened since then with the concentration of an ever-increasing share
of global income and wealth at the top, in the hands of the 1% world's
richest people whose share of the global income (19%) is more than
double that of the bottom 50% (8%) according to the *World Inequality
Report 2022* produced by the Paris-based World Inequality Lab.[4]

3 HOW HAVE THE PLACES IN WHICH YOU HAVE LIVED AND WORKED INFLUENCED YOUR VIEW ON GLOBAL INEQUALITY?

The places where I have lived and worked as an adult are Beirut, Paris,
Berlin and now London. Lebanon is a country that has itself been characterised by high social inequality, in a part of the world that is deemed
to be the most unequal of all. Lebanon provides a window on the global
hierarchy: it was theatre to a civil war starting in 1975, which was in
part a proxy war between global and regional powers through Lebanese
and Palestinian forces. Lebanon was then invaded by its Israeli neighbour

[2] See World Bank GDP per capita data at https://data.worldbank.org/indicator/NY.
GDP.PCAP.CD.

[3] UNDP, Human Development Report 1992 (New York: Oxford University Press,
1992).

[4] Lucas Chancel et al., eds., *World Inequality Report 2022* (Paris: World Inequality
Lab). The inequality in wealth is, of course, much higher yet: the top 1% hold 38% of
global wealth whereas the bottom 50% hold only 2%.

in 1982 and the experience of invasion by a foreign state, backed by the USA, is a powerful reminder of the global balance of forces and the global interconnectedness of various types of interests.

My years in Paris were very formative regarding global social inequality. The bicentenary of the French Revolution in 1989 was the occasion of a large international mobilisation in Paris to counter the G7 summit held on 14–16 July of that year, near Paris. A massive demonstration ended on the Place de la Bastille, where a huge public concert took place. This was the second major international mobilisation against the globalisation of neoliberalism, which was still in its early phase during those years. The first occurred in Berlin in 1988 in protest against meetings of the International Monetary Fund and the World Bank. A decade later, the 1999 Seattle mass protests against the conference of the World Trade Organisation led to the birth of what has become known under the name of the Global Justice movement, usually described as anti-globalist by its detractors while key sections of the movement prefer to refer to themselves as alter-globalist, a perspective expressed by the slogan "Another World is Possible".

A key founder of the World Social Forum (aka the Global Justice Movement) was ATTAC, the Association for the Taxation of Financial Transactions and for Citizens' Action, founded in Paris in 1998. It was related to the international monthly *Le Monde diplomatique*, a publication that has been focusing on global inequalities for several decades. I worked with both during my Paris years, and I still write for *Le Monde diplomatique*. Finally, moving to London concentrated my academic focus on the impact on development of all aspects of globalisation, and therefore on global inequality as explained above (Fig. 1).

4   What Are the Main Historical Causes of Global Inequality?

The world has never been an egalitarian place, to start with: in the social sense, inequality is as old as human history; in the sense of inequality between large organised communities—what we call states—it starts with the emergence of the first such communities and the fight over territory and resources. On the other hand, the historical civilisational process has seen the development of struggles for equality against systems of rigid formal oppression such as slavery and serfdom. This struggle took religious forms over millennia until the modern era when "equality" became

Fig. 1 A view of the fort guarding the port of the island of Gorée, close to Dakar, Senegal. Gorée has become a symbol of the Atlantic slave trade, the crudest and cruellest manifestation of global inequality that sustained the rise of capitalism (Photograph taken by Gilbert Achcar)

one of the main demands of democratic revolutions—equality in rights and, to a lesser extent, social equality, in addition to equality among nations.

The struggle for social equality progressed sharply in correlation with the industrial revolution and the spread of capitalism, which introduced an unprecedented degree of social differentiation within societies along with massive misery in the initial phase of industrialisation. The severe crises of global capitalism during the first half of the twentieth century gave rise after the Second World War to a competition between two global systems claiming equality in its various meanings as a core part of their value systems. However far this might have been from the reality of both systems, there is no dispute that the three decades that followed 1945 witnessed a massive reduction of the social gap at the global level and within countries.[5]

In this sense, the surge in global inequality that has become such a major topic of attention in recent decades is actually a resurgence of the inequality trend that characterised earlier phases of capitalism. Since the 1980s, we have seen a rapidly widening social gap within countries as well as at the global level. The main historical cause of this resurgence is the neoliberal turn that triumphed globally in the 1980s and 1990s, discarding the Keynesian and developmentalist paradigms that had prevailed in market economies in the aftermath of 1945 as well as the bureaucratic "socialist" systems of Eastern Europe and China. This neoliberal paradigm has been in crisis since the Great Recession starting in 2007–2008, a crisis now considerably aggravated by the ongoing economic turmoil related to the COVID-19 pandemic.

5   What Are the Most Pressing Contemporary Challenges Concerning Global Inequality, and How Do We Deal with Them?

The answer to this question is at present heavily affected by the consequences of the severe twin global crises of the pandemic and its socioeconomic consequences. Both crises have considerably widened the gap between the world rich and poor as well as between rich and poor countries. The huge numbers of poor and lower-income people in most "developing" and "least developed" countries of the Global South are very much disadvantaged in facing the pandemic compared to the overall situation in most "developed" countries of the geopolitical West in general, and to the global rich, including the rich in their own countries, in particular.

Likewise, the socioeconomic impact of what the IMF called the Great Lockdown[6] has sharply increased social inequality at the global level and within countries.[7] Hundreds of millions of people are expected to have permanently lost their pre-pandemic jobs by the end of the first pandemic

---

[5] See Chancel et al., eds., *World Inequality Report 2022*, among other sources.

[6] IMF, *World Economic Outlook: The Great Lockdown* (Washington: IMF, April 2020).

[7] Gilbert Achcar, "The Great Lockdown Hits the Third World Hard", *Le Monde diplomatique*, November 2020.

year, while several hundreds of millions are expected to have gone below the poverty line, with victims of gender and race discrimination being the most affected in both cases. Since the beginning of the pandemic, a few private corporations in sectors such as health, e-commerce, communications and entertainment have seen their profits go sky-high. These contradictory impacts of the crisis mean that the global rich-poor gap will certainly reach a peak at the onset of the 2020s compared with any previous period since 1945.

It has now become usual to liken the devastating impact of the ongoing pandemic to what the world did endure in the aftermath of the First World War, with the 1918 flu pandemic and the economic crisis that culminated in 1929 with the Great Depression. This huge crisis led to a second, even more devastating, global war. The world managed, however, to overcome that terrible first half of the twentieth century with a progressive programme of reconstruction and social reorganisation along with development of the welfare state, a programme funded by a much more equitable taxation of income and wealth than the current one. As a result, the world went through three decades of the fastest development it has ever experienced, along with a sharp reduction in global social inequality.

There will be no harmonious and successful overcoming of the ongoing global crisis without a new shift towards a social and economic paradigm that puts people before profits and is geared towards a massive increase in welfare and a sharp reduction of social and other global inequalities.

The Inertia of Hierarchies: Class, Caste, Race, Gender

Landscapes of Hierarchy

Dilip Menon

1   What Is Your Background and How Did You Become Interested in Global Inequality?

I was born in an India that was 17 years from the midnight hour of independence. My father was a civil servant, inducted into the civil services a year before the British left the shores of India. We grew up with the afterglow of decolonization, a perception of global inequality, and a sense of connectedness with other places in Asia, Africa, Latin America, and the Caribbean that had undergone a historical experience of domination and the entrenchment of inequality. This acquired a sharper edge with the Cold War, Vietnam, and the structural adjustment policies of the World Bank that sought to shape the world in the interests of Europe and America. In the metros of India, the perception of inequality was more intimate. Poverty was around us, we lived cheek by jowl with it. Even though the first generation after independence was characterized by austerity among the middle classes, a tightening of the belt that was a continuation of the war years, there was a vast gulf between the

D. Menon (✉)
University of Witwatersrand, Johannesburg, South Africa
e-mail: Dilip.Menon@wits.ac.za

C. O. Christiansen et al. (eds.), *Talking About Global Inequality*,
https://doi.org/10.1007/978-3-031-08042-5_12

older elites and those struggling to find employment within an economy growing at a glacial pace.

In 1957, the state of Kerala became the first region in the world to elect a communist government to power. As Malayalis from Kerala (the linguistic reorganization of states in 1956 meant that Kerala was a state of mainly speakers of the language Malayalam), we were conscious that we were from a special place. The major plank of the newly elected government was land redistribution and a generation of political and social mobilization meant that the program of land to the tiller was achieved with minimum fuss. My parents, both from the landowning gentry, were absolutely clear in their minds that this was what was needed. My father felt that without the albatross of land around his neck he could move on educationally and professionally. My mother had a more moral point of view; it was as if the weight of privilege and oppression had been lifted from her shoulders and she could live with a free conscience. As children, we grew up with a distaste for inherited privilege of any kind; a strong middle-class ethic which stressed that only that which we earned through our own labor was ours. Neither of my parents had any inheritance to fall back upon and they saw this as just. This may have been special to them, but we grew up thinking this was natural.

It was at school, at Delhi University, and subsequently while teaching in India, that the issue of caste inequality and the iniquitous depriving of the humanity of our fellow Indians became clearer. Teaching at Hyderabad University in the 1990s I encountered Dalit students (I had never studied with a Dalit student at school or college) who maintained a distance from me and would cower at a friendly touch. However, they were reading widely. Apart from the Dalit intellectual B.R. Ambedkar, they (and soon I too) were reading black American thinkers like WEB du Bois, Richard Wright, Angela Davis, and Malcolm X. The doxa at most universities in the 1990s was Marxism and reading thinkers on Latin American like André Gunder Frank and Paulo Freire was seen as required. We could see around us the effects of both the fundamental inequality and violence of caste-d life in India as much as the continuation of economic and political policies of the World Bank and IMF that still subjugated the global south. It didn't require much sensitivity or a leap of imagination to see that we lived in a landscape of inequality: local as much as global.

2   WHAT IS GLOBAL INEQUALITY?

At one level, there is the simple fact that societies everywhere are unequal. It is a matter of degree. There are no societies that are equal, except for perhaps small societies in Melanesia or Polynesia and this too is a matter of theorizing. Which is what led the American anthropologist Joel Robbins to say that inequality is a desolate half of a concept, given that it is posited against a largely non-existent equality.[1] I tend to think with the negotiation of hierarchy in all societies and find the French structuralist anthropologist Louis Dumont's comparative work extremely useful for this. In his trilogy on hierarchy, egalitarianism and individualism in Europe and South Asia, Dumont tried to step beside the easy binaries of opposing social ideologies in the East and West: of *homo hierarchicus* versus *homo aequalis*. He argued that if one put aside the conceits of modernity, all societies were characterized by both hierarchy and egalitarianism.[2] That said, while there are specific inequalities like caste in India, and race in the USA, which inflect the idea of democracy and hyphenate it—caste democracy and racial democracy—there is also a global political economy that determines trajectories of inequality within and between countries.

As a historian I think about existing global inequality as a result of 500 years of European colonialism that created a global paradigm of relating to peoples, nature and resources in general. In that sense, while not convinced of the idea of the Anthropocene (which implicates all of humanity), I am equally skeptical of the idea of the Capitalocene, because the creation of an unequal relation to humans and nature begins much before capitalism. In his superb essay *The Nutmeg's Curse*, Indian writer Amitav Ghosh goes back to early colonialism—the *conquistadores*, the genocide of the native Americans, Dutch atrocities in Southeast Asia—and an attitude to nature as merely an object of exploitation that displaced visions of the world in which a human is part of a larger landscape of animals, plants, and ancestors. The idea of dispensable humans and

---

[1] Joel Robbins, "Equality as a Value: Ideology in Dumont, Melanesia and the West," *Social Analysis: The International Journal of Social and Cultural Practice*, 36 (1994): 21–70.

[2] Louis Dumont, *Homo Hierarchicus: The Caste System and Its Implications* (Chicago: Chicago University Press. 1980); *Essays on Individualism: Modern Ideology in Anthropological Perspective* (Chicago: Chicago University Press, 1992).

visions is central to the instituting of hierarchies of value that under-gird inequality everywhere.[3] The East Asia expert Mark Driscoll provides another historical gloss with his idea of climate caucasianism which too emphasizes the effects of Western colonialism.[4] We live with the conse-quences of a paradigm generated by the particular globalization that colonialism instituted which built upon and entrenched local hierarchies and perpetuated hierarchies in the name of a civilizing mission and ideas of global freedom.

Global inequality is manifested in making the world open to and safe for capital. This was manifested in the 1980s with structural adjustment policies, in Chile led by natives educated in American universities like Chicago, and an alignment with neoclassical economics in Africa through expressed preferences for particular economists and organizations.[5] It also allowed for an equating of national good administration with economic practices that favored the free unhindered passage of Euramerican capital: the deposition of Allende's "socialist" government being an example of this. Policies of global south cooperation or import substitution were treated as autarkic romanticism. This has meant over the years that given local differences of articulation, attacks on farmers (subordinating local agrarian economies to the imperatives of PepsiCo or Monsanto); on indigenous groups (the invasion of lands with rich mineral resources whether in the Amazon, Australia, or Odisha); and the poor more gener-ally (poverty as a matter of failure of individual character) have become the global discourse. Globalization has become the practice of colonialism through other means. It has also meant that indigenous capitalists have access to this global network, so Indian firms like Adani and Vedanta perform a predatory mining capitalism in Australia, Africa, and India and act as the front for politically discredited Western operators like BHP who are now seen as rapacious asset strippers. Global inequality is also mani-fested in the offshoring of wealth and transnational flows of capital that

[3] Amitav Ghosh, *The Nutmeg's Curse: Parables for a Planet in Crisis* (Delhi: Penguin, 2021).

[4] Mark W. Driscoll, *The Whites are Enemies of Heaven: Climate Caucasianism and Asian Ecological Protection* (Durham: Duke University Press, 2020).

[5] T. Mkandawire, "The Spread of Economic Doctrine and Policymaking in Postcolonial Africa," *African Studies Review*, 57, 1 (2014): 171–198.

are not subject to national regimes of taxation (a problem, the resolution of which is central to much of Thomas Piketty's work).[6]

3 HOW HAVE THE PLACES IN WHICH YOU HAVE LIVED AND WORKED INFLUENCED YOUR VIEW ON GLOBAL INEQUALITY?

After an undergraduate degree in Delhi in 1983, I left to study at Oxford, before moving on to Cambridge to complete my PhD and stay on as a Research Fellow. It was a period of eight formative years in England. The United Kingdom was trying during that period—1984 to 1992—to come to terms with its decline in the wake of decolonization. Economic dislocation and a heightened racism went hand in hand with the military adventurism of the invasion of Falklands Islands. Being an Indian ("Paki") in England one was immediately made conscious of the pecking order of race and how an imperiled whiteness still carried the power to define others. Coming from the upper echelons of Indian society, and largely unaware of prejudice or the contempt of others, being the brunt of a crude racism made me aware of the larger landscapes of power and hierarchy, and of caste prejudices at home that I had largely ignored. At the same time, being part of anti-racism groups like the City of London anti-apartheid group and demonstrating against apartheid in South Africa at Trafalgar Square between 1986–1990, made me aware that the fight against prejudice was a global one.

More important than my sporadic personal involvement in such political activity was my perception of the epistemological backwardness of Oxbridge in terms of understanding the wounds that empire had inflicted on the colonies. British history was largely taught as a triumphalist internal narrative of increasing wealth, the growth of adult suffrage and the rise of England as a world power. That this was premised on colonialism and slavery was never reckoned for. Courses in the History Department such as the Rise of the West, European Expansion (the West and the Rest) were about an abstract narrative of the unfurling of the flag of freedom in darkened spaces; the function of empire seemed to have been the spread of enlightenment. Apart from this was the risible fact

---

[6] Thomas Piketty, *Capital and Ideology* (Cambridge, Mass.: Harvard University Press, 2020), p. 670.

that not one English historian of Asia or Africa knew an Asian or African language and worked only with the colonial archive. Expertise in indigenous languages was not deemed necessary and my cohort's knowledge of Indian languages (most of us had come from India to do our PhDs in the mother ship) was seen as merely an autobiographical fact rather than a pedagogical advantage. This was the fundamental fact of power. Native histories did not matter except as chapters in the narrative of the Empire's luminescence. Epistemological inequality—the overwhelming paradigm that "native" knowledge did not exist and therefore did no matter—was blunt and brutal in its articulation.

After returning to India in 1992, I traveled out again to the USA to teach at Yale in 1995, another bastion of privilege and forgetfulness. That the USA had been a former colony like India was too far back in the past for it to matter to anyone. However, what was even more shocking was the unawareness among most students and academics that I met of America's violent past of genocide of Amerindians and its current one of racial hierarchy at home and imperial intervention abroad. Not that those I spoke with didn't know, but that they saw it as a necessary violence that underlay the ultimate benevolence of American democracy and its exceptionalism. Yet again, I was reminded of the Hegelian insight that the master needed to know little about the slave. I taught a course on India which was an option, one largely attended by sentimental students of Indian origin who were largely unaware of their privilege and wholly uninterested in the social hierarchies of both India and the USA. Ideas of ineffable merit trumped a persistent history of racial violence; directed largely against the black community.

Moving to South Africa in 2009 to teach and being amid the #RhodesMustFall, #FeesMustFall, and #decolonize education agitations from 2015 onward, this question of a global pedagogy undergirded by the dichotomy of northern theory, southern fact was in the forefront.[7] My discomfort in Euramerican University spaces finally found a resolution in the realization that the most fundamental global inequality was the fact that those of us from the global south did not have an independent intellectual standpoint to understand the phenomenon. Education was the cultivation of an amnesia about the knowledge and traditions of intellection in the global south, as if freedom and emancipation were

---

[7] Dilip M. Menon, "Introduction," in Dilip M. Menon (edt), *Changing Theory: Concepts from the Global South* (London: Routledge, 2022).

Fig. 1 Installation by artist Riyas Komu titled *Fourth World* (2019), located in the Nirox Foundation Sculpture Garden, Johannesburg, South Africa. It shows four plinths of different heights facing the cardinal directions with statues of B.R. Ambedkar (1898–1951), the architect of the Indian constitution and Dalit intellectual. The artist was invited by the Center for Indian Studies in Africa, University of Witwatersrand, of which Dilip Menon is Director, and the idea of the installation was to suggest the necessity of conversations on caste and race in India and Africa (Photograph taken by Dilip Menon)

available only within the philosophies of the West. The political economy of publication and employment meant that the Euramerican University and publishing machine determined the frames and concepts of inquiry and one had to break free (Fig. 1).

4   What Are the Main Historical Causes of Global Inequality?

I have mentioned earlier the histories of neo-colonialism and the perpetuation of subordinate spaces even after decolonization, as spaces conducive to the free flow of capital. A further fact to be noted is the modular form of the nation-state that emerged in Asia and Africa in the wake of decolonization. These territorial entities premised on lines drawn in the dust for the administrative convenience and partition of spheres of influence among the imperial powers, ironically became the objects of worship among an emergent nationalist elite. These shadow lines (as Amitav Ghosh has termed them) effaced the histories of movement of peoples that had preceded as also continued beyond the end of empire and the formation of nations.[8] The idea of citizenship has as its underside the idea of the migrant, refugee, and stranger; those who do not belong. Given the natural flows of people from spaces of war, underdevelopment, and ecological change to more stable zones, the nation-state became the guarantor of economic and political stability creating a space of a "legitimate" economy that would work for international capital. Given that much of the cheap labor force is located in the global south, the nation-state buttressed by international law and global finance secures pliant and cheap labor.

One of the major rationales of the Cold War was the buttressing of nation-states and compliant indigenous elites against the emergence of democratic forms of government that would better serve local visions of an equitable politics. The deposition of the elected government of Mossadegh in Iran in 1953 and its replacement by the monarchy of the Shah; the assassination of Patrice Lumumba in the Congo by the CIA in 1961, the overthrow of the socialist government of Salvador Allende in Chile in 1974, and numerous coups and shenanigans by the former imperial powers and the USA, created a landscape of compromised nation-states that worked in the interest of international economic and political interests.[9] Nation-states and their elected governments have become the means to access the resources—environmental, ecological, and human—across the world and authoritarian governments have been tolerated, buttressed, and instituted to ensure an unhindered access to resources. We live in an age of the breakdown of Cold War structures—in the Arab world and north Africa from 2011 on—and the consequences of the untrammeled exploitation of resources by Europe and America that has resulted in climate change and its consequences. War and the

[8] Amitav Ghosh, *The Shadow Lines: A Novel* (Boston: Houghton Mifflin, 2005).

[9] "Patrice Lumumba: The most Important Assassination of the twentieth century," *The Guardian*, 20 January 2011 (https://www.theguardian.com/global-development/poverty-matters/2011/jan/17/patrice-lumumba-50th-anniversary-assassination (accessed 20 December 2021).

savaging of the environment has precipitated a large-scale movement of people across the globe as refugees, with nation-states expected to play a policing function.

Alongside the rhetoric of the integrity of nation-states is the cold fact that this is accompanied by the untrammeled flows of transnational capital across borders and frontiers. Triumphalist discourses of globalization and "the flat world" hide the entrenchment of global inequality and the cheapening of the lives of labor as much as the rights of indigenous people. Alongside the history of colonialism is the more contemporary history of the emergence of the nation as a natural form: a continuation of colonial relations through other means. The inability of nations to cooperate in regulating the drain of capital from their shores is evidence of this political form being a mere convenience for larger economic forces. Citizens increasingly experience the nation-state in its authoritarian forms through its generation of bare life, and pastoral care is very little in evidence. The recent abandonment of labor in India during the COVID- induced lockdown, followed by the wholescale cancelation of labor laws preceding the return of labor to work putatively in the interests of productivity is an indication of the argument that I have made in this essay.

5   What Are the Most Pressing Contemporary Challenges Concerning Global Inequality, and How Do We Deal with Them?

Given the fact of global warming, climate change, and the destruction of the environment in the interests of global capital, the first challenge is to create a more equitable international legal system in which all nations can be brought to account. As of now countries like the USA are not signatory to, nor bound by international law ranging from war crimes to resource use. The inequality of access to resources, that some continue to consume with impunity, is the first challenge.

The second challenge is to regulate the offshoring of profits by companies and individuals; where profits made off the exploitation of resources and cheap labor in one space are not ploughed back into reinvestment in that space. Piketty among others has argued for a transnational tax regime to resolve this crisis. Crony capitalism has become the hallmark of many nations in the global south, an unholy alliance between states and rapacious capitalists: for example, the corporate families of the Adanis, Ambanis, and Aggarwals of India.

With the financialization of capital and the dominance of the IT sector, the question remains of the generation of employment which is not restricted to the numbing routines of the service industry, nor the damage done by the exploitation of cheap labor. Amid the triumphal rhetoric of the fourth industrial revolution, what is forgotten is that for those who labor in the sweatshops of Asia, it is almost as if the era of the first industrial revolution has returned with no labor regulations, poor pay, and hazardous conditions of work.

Experiences of Inequality from India, a Sociobiographical View

Krishna Swamy Dara

1 WHAT IS YOUR BACKGROUND AND HOW DID YOU BECOME INTERESTED IN GLOBAL INEQUALITY?

I was born in a town called Guntur in the erstwhile state of Andhra Pradesh, South India, in the year 1974. My family belonged to the lower-middle-class Dalit group. Dalits are untouchables, a hugely marginalized section of India's population which was and is inflicted with various forms of social violence by the rest of society. My childhood was mostly growing up in the evangelist spirit of my maternal grandparents. They lived in a slum which was mostly composed of poor Dalit families living under extremely unhygienic and humiliating circumstances. Daily life was highly insecure and ridden with violence, for women in particular. Most families suffered from the alcoholism of men and intra-group violence with extreme masculinist ethos. This pain and suffering are etched in my memory even to this day.

K. S. Dara (✉)
Jamia Millia Islamia (Central University), New Delhi, India
e-mail: ksdara@gmail.com

C. O. Christiansen et al. (eds.), *Talking About Global Inequality*,
https://doi.org/10.1007/978-3-031-08042-5_13

My father was one of the lucky ones who could educate himself with the support of other educated relatives and managed to secure a government job. After this, my predicament changed. I dwelled in two different worlds: I spent my regular days in a middle-class colony, where things were more respectable and tidier, and weekends with my grandparents. As a very young boy, I preferred the world of my grandparents to my middle-class neighborhood. Kindness, care, and concern were values inculcated by them in me, and I think they are still the dominant values in the large sections of Dalits from this region. Christianity meant this to them.

These two worlds got contrasted as my father moved to the city (Hyderabad). Like most kids in those times, I spent a month or more with my grandparents in the summer holidays. In the city of Hyderabad, I changed schools many times until I landed in a Hindu philosophy-oriented school, where I finished my schooling. The values at home and the values at school contrasted drastically. The school environment, which was largely dominated by upper castes (both classmates and teachers), aimed to promote a kind of perfectionism and elitism that tend to see others as inferiors, including oneself when one does not match these meritocratic criteria. Stereotyping and stigmatizing others was common practice, particularly against women, lower castes, and Muslims. Jokes about these groups are common among school students and sometimes triggered by the teachers too. Cultures that justify and naturalize inequality exist and have a long history (Fig. 1).

2   What Is Global Inequality?

Social and economic inequality is a global phenomenon. We come to realize this when we understand more and more about other societies and countries apart from our own. In other words, societies that claim to be egalitarian and just (particularly Western countries) are ridden with high levels of poverty, inequities, and injustice. Comparing poorer nations with rich ones also shows huge discrepancies in terms of social and economic wellbeing. The concern about global inequality has a long history since Marx's *Capital*, and criticisms about imperialism and colonialism now have a considerable history. As I come from a deeply (and unlike any other) hierarchal society, which also witnessed colonial exploitation and domination, the issues of global inequality are part of our history. It is inculcated in our education early on. Most Indian history textbooks in

Fig. 1 Site of children begging on the streets of Delhi. Mostly these children come from lower class/caste families who live on the streets without proper housing and hygienic conditions. This betrays the promise of equality that the Indian Constitution and society openly champion (Photograph by Krishna Swamy)

schools talk of colonialism and the struggle against it. It is also called nationalist history.

By global inequality, I mean the huge difference that exists between populations all over the planet in terms of economic wealth. Although resources are distributed throughout the planet, the benefits from these resources are unfairly unequal. Those with an economic surplus can exploit and enjoy these resources exclusively. With these economic surpluses they can also exploit other humans, both physically and in terms of their talent. The effect is an exploitative environment that is deeply inhuman and horrific for the exploited. Apart from Marx, I am also deeply influenced by the political thought of John Rawls and his theory of justice. I find the application of his theories at the global level in the name of global justice very promising. The work of Thomas Pogge is also very promising in this regard.[1] Global justice and global inequality are related because inequality is understood as an unjust predicament.

3   How Have the Places in Which You Have Lived and Worked Influenced Your View on Global Inequality?

My experience at Jawaharlal Nehru University (1997–2006) was very enriching and also deeply disturbing. This is one of the top universities for the study of humanities in India. I studied political science as a subject, as I considered it the most relevant discipline for understanding the politics of society and for bringing change for the better. At first glance, the campus was one of the most overtly political and progressive, with students who counted as some of the best from India. However, although professors professed egalitarian and democratic values in the classroom, they practiced an extreme form of class/caste elitism informally. They promoted inequality and competition among students in the name of merit and hard work. Recommendation letters, personal interaction and encouragement and other networking opportunities were offered to their perceived favorites. Similarly, they overlooked students who were mostly coming from lower class and caste backgrounds, a typical strategy to promote opportunity hoarding.[2]

This forced me to think about the politics of this duplicity and the future of social justice. The campus also had a vibrant protest culture that encouraged free thinking and debate. It helped young students like me to get to know various dimensions of politics and social problems. As a left-leaning student, my intellectual concerns were opposed to Western domination. This was coupled with lectures on dependency theory and the concepts of center and periphery. Along with the works of Marx and Lenin, the work of Samir Amin was influential in my understanding of global inequality.

---

[1] Thomas Pogge and Keane Bhatt, "Thomas Pogge on Global Poverty," May 31, 2011, https://www.globalpolicy.org/social-and-economic-policy/global-injustice-and-ine quality/inequality-of-wealth-and-income-distribution/50272-thomas-pogge-on-global-pov erty.html. (Visited 19 December, 2021).

[2] See Charles Tilly, *The Politics of Collective Violence* (Cambridge, New York: Cambridge University. Press, 2008).

I also participated in protests against the domination of the United States and its allies in meddling with the politics and political economy of the Middle East. The American invasion of Iraq, with the duplicitous intention of opposing dictatorship and bringing democracy, was a way to exploit the natural resources of the region. I still hold on to such a view but with many reservations. The policies of the World Bank, the International Monetary Fund, and other international organizations are responsible for creating economic dependency. Control and monopolizing of trade by rich nations are direct causes of impoverishment of resource-rich countries in Africa, Asia, and Southern America.

4   WHAT ARE THE MAIN HISTORICAL CAUSES OF GLOBAL INEQUALITY?

As a social scientist, I tend to see the problem of global inequality in interdisciplinary and intersectional terms. Global inequality, or any inequality in human society, is a product of human thought and should therefore be seen in historical and ideological terms. Without going into the debates between materialists and idealists, we can safely say à la Hegel that material reality is an interpretation of the human mind, which is itself historical, hence material too.

Historically, colonialism—with its ideology of racial and national superiority—has produced this inequality where mostly the colonies end up being dependent on the colonizer to a large extent for economic and cultural support. International trade mechanisms and its institutions like the International Monetary Fund and the World Bank developed from these unjust exploitations and continue to perpetuate these inequities although the erstwhile colonies are now independent politically. The economic systems in my view are largely unjust and exploitive toward the poorer nations.

Although we have a high-flown rhetoric for democracy and human rights, in practice they work as a façade for perpetuating deeper disparities and discriminations like American interventions both militarily and economically in poor countries in the name of democracy. Here, I want to bring the attention of the reader to how the global elite, largely located in the so-called Western world, have managed to accommodate third-world elites (both economic and cultural). This accommodation mutually helps the continued dominance by the Western elite globally, and domination by the third-world elite locally. Indian elites are thus part of this rotten compromise. The ideologies of capitalism, racism, sexism, patriarchy and casteism are supported by subtle, seemingly innocuous ideologies of meritocracy, ableism, perfectionism and legalism.[3] One of the sources of inequality is religion, which tends to promote fatalism and inaction in terms of tackling inequality (I am aware of various forms of liberation theologies, but they largely tend to fail to change common sense notions). Justifications for retaining privilege and advantages as God-given (part of god's plan) or one's karma (work of moral effort in a previous life) play a role in society's acceptance of social and economic inequality. This is particularly so in the Third World.

5   What Are the Most Pressing Contemporary Challenges Concerning Global Inequality, and How Do We Deal with Them?

My work on Gandhi on the relationship between religion and politics is to test the secular thesis in practice. Although I do not agree with him on every count, some of his arguments like "there is enough for everyone's need but not for everyone's greed" makes perfect sense.[4] For Gandhi, colonialism was an expression of human greed and its impulse to promote human consumption. Even capitalism is another form of human greed (this time of profit) that exploits both international labor and domestic labor, and it is the main source of inequality at a global level. Gandhian politics of minimalism for daily sustenance, although environmentally friendly, can produce a culture of celebrating poverty. The culture of poverty has deep roots in Indian philosophical traditions which had a deleterious effect on the Indian psyche.

This brought me to the politics and work of Dr. B.R. Ambedkar, after which I decided to focus my Ph.D. on his political philosophy. He was a highly educated and trained intellectual. His works touch upon many fields like sociology, history, economics, finance, and politics. My work focused on his political thought on the rights of minorities in a

---

[3] Daniel Markovits, *The Meritocracy Trap* (London: Penguin Books, 2020); Judith N. Shklar, *Legalism: Law, Morals and Political Trials* (Cambridge, Mass.: Harvard University Press, 1986).

[4] Jeffrey D Sachs, "The Earth Provides Enough to Meet Everyone's Needs," *The National*, March 2, 2011, https://www.thenationalnews.com/opinion/comment/the-earth-provides-enough-to-meet-everyone-s-needs-1.426562. (Visited 19 December 2021).

democracy. His early Ph.D.-based book remains a main study of political economy, in which he deals with the problem of currency standard. The work was published in the year 1923 with the title "The Problem of The Rupee: its origin and its solution."[5] In this work, he argued that the Indian economy was advanced and flourishing before the advent of British colonialism. All in all, B.R. Ambedkar argued that rich India was impoverished by the British colonial policies. Apart from colonial exploitation and imperialism, B.R. Ambedkar's work also deals with class exploitation in socio-economic terms. He argues that just as the rule of one nation over another is immoral and unacceptable, so is the rule of one class over another class. One of his main suggestions for dealing with all kinds of injustices including global inequality is not just to see inequality in purely economic terms, but (à la Gramsci) to see them as cultural hegemonies without ignoring the economic or material aspect. There is an urgent need to introduce and see democracy as a way of life à la John Dewey, to question the vulgar aspects of modernity and capitalism, to deal with greed à la Gandhi, and create compassion for fellow creatures (including humans) à la Buddha.

[5] Marxists.org, "B. R. Ambedkar," https://www.marxists.org/archive/ambedkar/index. htm. (Visited 19 December 2021).

Writing About Poverty and Caste as a Novelist and Cultural Critic

S. Shankar

1   WHAT IS YOUR BACKGROUND AND HOW DID YOU BECOME INTERESTED IN GLOBAL INEQUALITY?

I am from India from a salaried middle-class family, though I lived in different parts of the world growing up, including Germany (in the 1960s) and Nigeria (in the 1970s). In a sense, I have always been interested in global inequality because of the variety of societies I have experienced. Coming from a salaried middle-class family meant that our sense of security was very much connected to my father's job (as a diplomat for newly independent India) rather than the vicissitudes of the market or the inheritance of accumulated wealth. We were petty bourgeois in the language of classical Marxism. I remember distinctly a sense of somewhat reduced circumstances when my father retired, which happened to coincide roughly with when I entered college in 1981. It was clear to me that economic security in the future was not something to be taken for granted. It was something to be worked for, possibly by landing a salaried job like my father's. That in some ways I chose not to

S. Shankar (✉)
Department of English, University of Hawai'i at Mānoa, Honolulu, HI, US
e-mail: subraman@hawaii.edu

follow that path—choosing rather to be a writer and a scholar—is another story. And in the end, I became not that different from my father in many ways, supporting myself via a salaried position at an American university. The more things change the more they remain the same?

At the same time, my family is upper caste and that is a different experience of inequality, since the relationship of caste to class is a real but not neat one. If my class privilege was significant but not entirely secure, my caste privilege was considerable. As a young man exposed to radical thought, I was very much aware of this privilege, but it was not until much later—in graduate school in the US in the late 1980s and early 1990s—that I acquired the terminology of "cultural capital" via which to understand this caste privilege. To put the matter succinctly: regardless of my class status, my life has been marked from the beginning by the cultural capital (the privileged social networks, perceptions, and identifications) that accrues to upper-caste status. This cultural capital has surely played a very significant role in my ability to navigate an unequal world.

My background is crucial to my interest in global inequality. Ironically, the privilege of travel has taught me to think comparatively about a global lack of privilege. As a writer, I began composing short stories and poems about the poor. Later, poverty and inequality came to be thematized directly in two of my three novels (*A Map of Where I Live* and *Ghost in the Tamarind*, the latter of which sets out to tell the story of caste inequality in South India); and became in a more indirect way the subject of my scholarship in postcolonial studies (though, finally I am now more directly writing a scholarly book on representations of the poor in literature and film).

2   WHAT IS GLOBAL INEQUALITY?

I want to say: difficult to answer precisely. I will say: the differentially dis-/empowering experience of the world within a community of human beings spread out across the globe. As an ethical and intellectual challenge, the question is meaningful only when understood in a socially significant way, as a question linked to the interrogation of the capacity for self-actualization (however you understand this term) of human beings within communities. Historically, not all societies have understood in the same way what it means to self-actualize, that is, what it means for a person to live to the fullest. Does self-actualization mean to experience without limits? Or, rather, does it mean to live a life of solicitude for others? And what is the role of society in enabling such self-actualization? Viewed in the context of such questions, *global inequality* is meaningful only when the word *inequality* has a globally generalizable signification in relation to (social) power structures and self-actualization. To illustrate: the inequality of height may signify if you are a professional basketball player, but it does not signify in a globally generalizable way.

So far, so good (maybe). The difficulties arise when we move beyond this highly abstracted level of definition and begin an inquiry into causes, effects, histories, varieties, and more. And then there are the difficulties to do with the very posing of the question. If there are culturally variant notions of inequality, then what does it mean to inquire into global inequality? To pose the question differently: whose inequality are we placing at the center—treating as a category capable of universalization—when we ask after *global* inequality? In some ways, a globalizing world—a world in which a pandemic like COVID-19 originates in one place and then rages across the world affecting the global community of human beings in dis-/empowering ways—itself provides an answer to the question. Inequality that has the most widespread resonance is the most global. On the other hand, there is no need that we should accept the answer the world imposes on us. The world routinely propagates—imposes on us—modes of thinking that perpetuate the status quo. Might new light on inequality be shed by willfully utopian, perhaps anti-global, perspectives? The merits of counterfactual thinking should not be discounted. Whose global inequality, indeed.

3   How Have the Places in Which You Have Lived and Worked Influenced Your View on Global Inequality?

As I have said, I grew up in Germany and Nigeria as well as India. If I learned caste in India, I learned (I realize now) race in Germany and Nigeria, and that too in different ways—as a brown child in a white and a black country respectively. I was older when I was in Nigeria—in a way, I came of age there. From my life in Nigeria, I have carried an abiding interest in race and in Africa, to which I have returned as an adult and about whose literature I have written extensively. It was difficult to be a young person with intellectual interests coming of age in Nigeria and

India in the 1970s without being attuned to the language of development through which these countries were understood (now it is all about emerging markets). It was difficult to walk or drive past slums with my background of living in different countries and not grow interested in the "wealth of nations."

I moved to the United States when I was twenty-five to go to graduate school, and now I have lived more than half my life in that country, albeit with extended stretches back "home" in India. That has also been an "influence." To experience the American empire from within the belly of the beast is instructive. At its most immediate, I am taught every time I travel between the United States and India about the vast differences in consumption and also the ways in which this consumption is to a large extent beyond the voluntaristic—that is, it is structural. You can make enlightened personal choices with regard to consumption in the Unites States and still end up participating in a highly resource-intensive lifestyle. The flip side of this observation is also true. You have a significant minority of people in countries like India who personally consume on a scale comparable to the majority of people in countries like the United States but whose carbon footprint would be lower because of the structural differences between the countries. In this way, I have come to think more and more of how consumption—very broadly construed—is a hinge concept linking economic inequality with climate change and planetary degradation.

Of course, economic inequality is not the only form of inequality. Racialized—and also racist—forms of thought are as significant in the United States as caste is in India. More recently, I have grown interested in thinking comparatively regarding forms of inequality—economic or racial or caste-based—as a way of trying to understand something more foundational about inequality as such. Some of this interest has found expression in my recent work on caste (such as in my co-edited book *Caste and Life Narratives*).

4   What Are the Main Historical Causes of Global Inequality?

Understanding *global* as a rough synonym for the planetary, we might say the main causes, to put the matter at its broadest, are colonialism and capitalism. Colonialism was and is, among other things, a system of resource extraction and redistribution for the benefit of one part of the globe and to the detriment of another by way of a deployment of difference based on race, ethnicity, and cultural alterity. Capitalism is colonialism's twin—both cause and effect of it. It is different from colonialism in being the name for an alternative set of processes and mechanisms centered on the subjection of everything—or as much as possible at any given moment—to the rule of the commodity. As I argued in my first critical book *Textual Traffic: Colonialism, Modernity, and the Economy of the Text*, at an existential level it is not possible to ascribe priority to one over the other (that is, to colonialism over capitalism or vice versa).[1] Colonialism and capitalism are best thought of as coeval in their emergence.

To be sure, these comments make sense only when contemplating *globe* as a rough synonym for *planet*, and when we are trying to map inequality in this planetary sense. From a different perspective, gender and sexual difference, for example, are as much if not more pervasive in being commandeered for the generation of human inequality. Conceptual rigor requires that when we contemplate inequality, we keep context and intersecting issues in clear view—unless we are engaged with a broader philosophical discussion of the very conditions of possibility for any equality as such. Since I am not a philosopher, I tend to be more interested in the contextual and intersectional dimensions of global inequality.

5   WHAT ARE THE MOST PRESSING CONTEMPORARY CHALLENGES CONCERNING GLOBAL INEQUALITY, AND HOW DO WE DEAL WITH THEM?

Is it useful to rephrase the question in the following way: what are the contemporary challenges concerning global *equality* (rather than *in*equality)? Equality before the law? Equality of opportunities? Equality of outcomes? Equality is a necessary and unavoidable orienting goal but its semantics are not self-evident, at least to my mind. (It is also worth asking whether *equivalence* is a more useful term than *equality*, but that is discussion for another day.) I have been working on a book on cultural representations of the poor in a global context. The scholarship

---

[1] S. Shankar, *Textual Traffic: Colonialism, Modernity, and the Economy of the Text* (New York: SUNY Press, 2001).

on poverty amply illustrates the (allegedly) vexed relationship between equality and destitution. The (neoliberal) argument that inequality may be the price to be paid by a society for freedom from destitution has often been made. The refutation of this claim is a great contemporary theoretical challenge concerning global inequality.

Another great challenge involves the struggle over inequality in relation to climate change and the planetary environmental crisis, both of which tend to trump every other concern in discussions of the future. Why bother thinking about inequality when there is a planet to save? This kind of apocalyptic thinking has always shoved aside more mundane matters of justice like persistent inequality. However, as I explore in a recent short story, inequality might very well survive the apocalypse.[2] There is certainly no guarantee that the unfolding costs of climate and environmental crisis will not be selectively displaced—as they already are—onto helpless populations through sustained systems of inequality. One hopes that an acute sense of shared doom will create the conditions to foster yet unimagined ideologies of equality. An outcome of equality, however, will still have to be the result of struggle, not inevitability.

[2] "Chennai Block South: Intrusion of Untouchables," *ISLE* 27.4 (Autumn 2020): 859–76.

Reflecting on My Experiences of Gender Inequality in Kenya and South Africa

Arabo K. Ewinyu

1   WHAT IS YOUR BACKGROUND AND HOW DID YOU BECOME INTERESTED IN GLOBAL INEQUALITY?

My initial interest in global inequality was sparked by following the proceedings of the Fourth Women Conference held in 1995 in Beijing, which was a major turning point in the international battle against gender inequality. As a ten-year old, it led me to question why women would require a separate forum to advocate for their rights, while men did not. During this conference, I also recall hearing men making several derogatory comments about "Beijing Women" and how you should be careful that the Kenyan female representatives did not return and "fill the heads of their women with these feminist ideas". Such rhetoric stood in sharp contrast with the highlights of female representatives attending different sessions, which were cast on the daily evening news. Although it took me years to contextualise and vocalise this, I realise now that this was my introduction to the fact that certain systemic inequalities existed within and across societies.

A. K. Ewinyu (✉)
University of the Witwatersrand, Johannesburg, South Africa
e-mail: arabo.ewinyu@wits.ac.za

C. O. Christiansen et al. (eds.), *Talking About Global Inequality*,
https://doi.org/10.1007/978-3-031-08042-5_15

123

I was born and raised in Nairobi, Kenya as the last child in a family of five girls, at a time when the boy child was favoured for the mere fact of being male. Kenya in the 1980s was a country in flux as various shifts occurred. Politically, the late President Daniel Moi survived a coup in 1982. Moi was limiting press and democratic freedom, making Kenya more autocratic. Economically, various structural adjustment policies had been instituted, resulting in mass privatisation, increasing unemployment and the expansion of precarious types of employment, as firms sought to reduce costs. This had direct bearing on family life, because increased poverty and despair served to strengthen very strong patriarchal beliefs and thoughts, as disenfranchised men sough to exert their authority in the allocation of household resources and in relationships with their wives.

In the late 1990s, I saw how such patriarchy led to young girls being ejected from schools to get married, to care for older and younger family members. Poorer homes focused meagre resources on the' education of male children. Personally, although I went to a progressive primary school, female students, including myself, were often pulled out of class to practise songs and dances to entertain visiting donors and other high ranking male guests.

In sharp contrast, within my own family, I could see how increased access to education across generations had changed the opportunities provided to me and all my sisters. My paternal grandmother, born in 1924 in rural Eastern Uganda, only had two years of schooling. Despite being widowed at a young age with two sons, she pushed my father to study and obtain post-high school training. My mother also qualified as a nurse. My sisters and I all attended university. In the course of three generations, the opportunities afforded to us were remarkably better. More generally, we now see the birth of fewer and healthier children, increased post-retirement savings, and greater freedom to pursue employment across various higher paying international labour markets.

The circumstances of my own family and upbringing, sparked my interest in studying economics in order to understand how inequality manifests itself and is perpetuated across generations, countries and genders—and to consider the types of interventions that can shift this trajectory. Hence, I completed an undergraduate degree, Bachelor of Science (economics), at Daystar University in Nairobi, Kenya in 2007, and worked for a year before undertaking my postgraduate studies at the University of the Witwatersrand in Johannesburg, South Africa.

2   What Is Global Inequality?

Global inequality refers to the divergence in the distribution of resources across various nations, and the impact this has on opportunities or individual outcomes' in poorer or less powerful countries.[1]

To understand global inequality, it is important to distinguish between inequality of outcomes and inequality of opportunities. The former is measured by metrics such as income, wealth, assets or expenditure. Income (or expenditure) inequality is the most commonly used measure of inequality in outcomes, and often compares the Gini coefficient of countries, based upon the incomes earned by individuals or households.[2]

Inequality of opportunities is measured by comparing health, education and human development outcomes by income group, or by examining access to basic services and opportunities. These differences are viewed as often being out of the individual's' control. These include gender, race or ethnicity, location of birth and other family characteristics for instance, the education level of your parents.[3]

Recent work in understanding inequality has focused on asset-based living standard indicators to measure multidimensional inequality. The approach is a combination of ownership to household assets and access to basic services.[4] This is a useful measure where data on income and/or expenditure are unavailable or difficult to access.

What makes me particularly interested in global inequality is that as a focal theme, inequality takes on different shapes across countries, regions and across various divides. It therefore requires a more nuanced understanding of the topic to observe global trends, and then understand how they become manifest at the local level.

[1] Era Dabla-Norris, Kalpana Kochhar, Nujin Suphaphiphat, Frantisek Ricka, and Evridiki Tsounta, *Causes and Consequences of Income Inequality: A Global Perspective* (Washington DC: International Monetary Fund, 2015).

[2] François Bourguignon and Marta Menéndez, *Inequality of Outcomes and Inequality of Opportunities in Brazil* (Washington, DC: World Bank, 2003).

[3] Paolo Brunori, Francisco H.G. Ferreira and Vito Peragine, "Inequality of Opportunity, Income Inequality, and Economic Mobility: Some International Comparisons", in E. Paus (edt.), *Getting Development Right* (New York: Palgrave Macmillan, 2013), pp. 85–115.

[4] Muna Shifa and Vimal Ranchhod, *Handbook on Inequality Measurement for Country Studies* (Cape Town: UCT 2019).

3   How Have the Places in Which You Have Lived and Worked Influenced Your View on Global Inequality?

In 2008, I left Kenya and moved to South Africa for postgraduate studies. These two countries have strongly influenced my view and perception of global inequality.

Growing up in Kenya after the Beijing 1995 conference, I was able to benefit from the myriad policies that were enacted to bridge the access and performance gender-based gap. This has made me a firm believer in the role of policy and education to reverse what sometimes feels like a pre-determined inequality path. Using fertility trends as an example, we see that the average woman in Kenya in 1982 had 7.2 children. In 2018, this number has more than halved to 3.5 births per woman.[5]

Living in South Africa, the most unequal country in the world, has also exposed me to visible inequalities across race, gender and space. On a daily basis I am confronted by the fact that the domestic helper who works in my house, spends almost an hour in a minibus to commute to my house and back to her own home.[6] Racial disparities are evident by the fact that the majority of the higher paid individuals across most formal workplaces are still male and white, with the majority of the lower skilled individuals being primarily female and African.[7]

The experience of living and working in South Africa has increased the scope of my knowledge and expectations, making me a more engaged and empathetic inequality researcher.

4   What Are the Main Historical Causes of Global Inequality?

Centuries of unequal progress has entrenched inequality. A key driver of this uneven progress is the history of colonisation, as colonised countries have seen their resources exploited and the benefits accruing only to the colonising country.

---

[5] "Fertility rate, total (births per woman)" last modified November 18, 2020, https://data.worldbank.org/indicator/SP.DYN.TFRT.IN?locations=BD-IN-SN-KE-ZA-CD-TZ. (Accessed 20 December, 2021).

[6] Andrew Kerr, "Tax (i) ing the Poor? Commuting Costs in South African Cities," *South African Journal of Economics*, 85, no. 3 (2017): 321–340.

[7] *20th Commission for Employment Equity Annual Report 2019–2020*. (Pretoria: The Department of Labour, 2020).

In pre-colonial time, land was a key asset that provided security to the family and a source of income, whether from the sale of produce or through the rearing of livestock. Traditional land tenure systems were displaced by the discriminatory land laws that often gave settlers access to prime land and surplus labour to work the land at little to no cost. Land inequality is a bedrock of "long-run persistent wealth and asset inequality."[8] Not only did land inequality affect wealth distribution in pre-colonial times, but also the types of post-colonial institutions that were developed. Following Kenya's independence in 1963, several violent tribal clashes have erupted, as displaced tribes fought with "outsiders" who they felt benefitted unfairly from unjust colonial land policies.[9] Particularly in election times, land ownership forms the basis of campaign manifestos for various political parties who, once elected, often ignore it.

Furthermore, such colonised nations have lacked the power and the requisite institutional capacity to meaningfully participate in trade and global supply chains post-independence. Consequently, this initial inequality between nations is now reinforced by the increasing role of technological advancement. In the last forty years, many countries have increasingly taken advantage of technological advancements to lower production costs, access foreign investment and gain access to global value chains, while other countries have largely missed out on this development.[10]

An additional downside to this technological shift is the impact on the labour market. Globalised labour markets are attractive and accessible to highly skilled individuals who enjoy greater mobility and wages. Low skilled individuals and unskilled workers are excluded from these high-paying, international jobs.

It is widely acknowledged that while increased technological advancements are good for human advancement and the eradication of societal

[8] Ewout Frankema, "The Colonial Roots of Land Inequality: Geography, Factor Endowments, or Institutions?" *The Economic History Review*, 63, no. 2 (2010): 418.

[9] Martin Shanguhyia and Mickie Mwanzia Koster, "Land and Conflict in Kenya's Rift Valley: Historical and Contemporary Perspectives", in T. Falola and E. Mbah (eds.), *Contemporary Africa* (New York: Palgrave Macmillan, 2014), pp. 191–223; Leighann Spencer, "Kenya's History of Political Violence: Colonialism, Vigilantes and Militias", *The Conversation*. September 28, 2017 https://theconversation.com/kenyas-history-of-politi cal-violence-colonialism-vigilantes-and-militias-83888. (Accessed 20 December 2021).

[10] UNDP, *Human Development Report 1999*. (New York: OUP, 1999).

ills such as poverty and certain diseases, the development of global technology firms such as Facebook, Apple and Amazon, to name a few, cannot continue unchecked as returns to a few individuals and investor firms is a source of widening income and wealth inequality.

5   What Are the Most Pressing Contemporary Challenges Concerning Global Inequality, and How Do We Deal with Them?

There are several issues which could be addressed, but I will focus on two. The first is the observed trend of declining poverty and rising inequality in some countries such as India and China. This results in income polarisation as the share of formerly poor and vulnerable are faced with a greater probability of falling back into poverty. At the middle to upper end of the income distribution, we observe significant gains to the share of income of these income groups.[11] Increasing access to opportunities such as education and health could result in greater gains for lower income individuals, and could with time result in greater returns to these groups.

Second, in some countries we observe the institutionalisation of inequality resulting in successive generations replicating previous trends. Examples include racial outcomes in countries such as South Africa and America. The same is also true of labour wage inequality as owners of firms continue to be richly remunerated relative to their employees, as evidenced in the growing disparity in the ratio of the CEO pay to the lowest earning employee.[12] Taking global unrest and rising unemployment into view, it is important to consider alternative forms of ownership and possibly restructuring the firm or the corporation. Some of these could include increased or mandatory worker representation on management boards in order to ensure that the interests of all relevant stakeholders are considered.

---

[11] Tony Addison, Jukka Pirttilä and Finn Tarp, "Inequality: Measurement, Trends, Impacts and Policies", *Review of Income and Wealth*, 63, no. 4 (2017): 603–607.

[12] "Massive R180 Million Payday for Naspers Boss" *Business Tech.* July 22, 2019. https://businesstech.co.za/news/business/330515/massive-r180-million-payday-for-naspers-boss/; "Meet the Retail Bosses who Earn Around R70,000 a Day" *Business Tech.* 7 October 2019 https://businesstech.co.za/news/wealth/344876/meet-the-retail-bosses-who-earn-around-r70000-a-day/ (both accessed 20 December 2021).

Global Resistances and Solidarities: A View from Nepal

Manushi Yami Bhattarai

1   What Is Your Background and How Did You Become Interested in Global Inequality?

I was born in 1986, in Kathmandu, Nepal which was then a Hindu Kingdom. During two hundred and forty years of Shah monarchy, our country has witnessed major political upheavals and revolts against autocratic regimes. I was only four years old when the 1990 People's Movement led to a constitutional monarchy and the restoration of a multi-party parliamentary democracy. My parents were political leaders and led the civil resistance movement. My father, Baburam Bhattarai, was the chairperson of United People's Front Nepal, and my mother, Hisila Yami, was the President of All Nepal Women's Association (Revolutionary). The Maoist People's War, an underground movement, was inspired by the Chinese revolution and guerilla warfare tactics. It was launched in 1996 by the Communist Party of Nepal (Maoist). My parents were at the very forefront of this movement, and went underground at the time of its inception, when I was ten years old. As an

M. Yami Bhattarai (✉)
Tribhuvan University, Kirtipur, Nepal
e-mail: manushiyb@gmail.com

only child of two prominent leaders wanted by the government for their extra-parliamentary activities, I was under constant surveillance by state intelligence agencies. Eventually, I too had to go into hiding. From 1996 and for the next nine years, I had to take shelter in different parts of Nepal, and mostly in India where I continued my education. I had witnessed the movement very closely, and it instilled a strong political consciousness in me from a young age.

In 2001, I formally joined the Maoist party, and helped organize Nepali migrant workers mostly in Faridabad and Delhi, India. After the Comprehensive Peace Accord was signed between the Government of Nepal and the Communist Party of Nepal (Maoist) in 2006, I returned to Kathmandu. While pursuing a Masters Degree in Political Science at Tribhuvan University, I was involved in the student's movement. I watched the transition of Nepal from an autocratic monarchial regime to becoming a Federal Democratic Republic. This was possible due to the sacrifices of thousands of people, mostly belonging to an economically and socially oppressed class, gender, caste, nationality/ethnicity, and region. In 2009, I got elected as the secretary of the student representative body of Tribhuvan University Central Campus. Presently, I am associated with the Socialist Party of Nepal, and work in the Kathmandu district and Bagmati Province, with a focus on gender and urbanization issues. Academically, my areas of interest include political theory, democracy, Marxism, political institutions, and constitutional studies.

Being born in a political family, I was exposed to a host of political ideas, activities, books, and personalities from a young age. These ideas were shaped largely by Marxian and communist traditions along with other philosophical and political traditions. Though both my parents were trained as architects and lived as an urban middle-class family, they worked with and for the downtrodden. Because of my upbringing, I was sensitive and perceptive about existing inequalities in Nepali society from a young age. It inculcated in me an outlook to see the unseen, hear the unheard, and resist all oppression. Furthermore, the years spent in different parts of India, and two years in the UK, made me insightful about the nature and impact of inequality among people, situated in similar conditions but across national boundaries. I also became more cognizant of inequality among countries, both regionally and globally (Fig. 1).

People gathered for a mass meeting called by the Naya Shakti Party Nepal in a village in Gorkha district in the run-up to the 2017 general elections. Manushi Yami Bhattarai was an active member of the party.

Fig. 1 People gathered for a mass meeting called by the Naya Shakti Party Nepal in a village in Gorkha district in the run-up to the 2017 general elections. Manushi Yami Bhattarai was an active member of the party. After a merger, the party is now called the Nepal Samajbadi Party or the Socialist Party of Nepal (Photograph taken by Manushi Yami Bhattarai)

After a merger, the party is now called the Janata Samajbadi Party or the People's Socialist Party Nepal; photograph taken by Manushi Yami Bhattarai.

2   What Is Global Inequality?

Global inequality is stark gaps in ownership, access and accumulation of resources and rights: economic, political, social, cultural, as well as environmental and ecological differences, between countries, and groups of people. These inequalities run both vertically and horizontally, as they are based upon class as well as upon region, gender, ethnicity, race, and caste. It is a highly unfair lopsided global phenomenon, as the gap among people and between countries is so extreme. The division is not natural, and nor did it occur accidentally. Rather, it is a deliberate man-made inequality based on exploitation, colonization, and domination. It is disproportionate, because the power and wealth of a handful of countries and individuals outweigh those of the rest of the world. It is a global phenomenon because of the nexus between states, institutions, markets, and actors that enable and reinforce such disparities, globally.

Economically, such a gap is seen in terms of land ownership, income, wealth, and other assets. For instance, in Nepal, 5% of the population control 37% of arable land, while 41.4% of the Tarai Dalits are landless.[1] Furthermore, it is astonishing that a human being can earn up to 20 times less for the exact same work in different countries for no fault of their own![2] Politically, a handful of countries exercise more power over the rest. The United States has excessive capacity to influence major global policies, such as those related to climate change which disproportionately affect regions like the Himalayas.

The poor, women, indigenous communities, Dalits, the youth, the queer community, immigrants, and the disabled, have disproportionate little share in political representation worldwide. This leads to an imbalance in the capacity to formulate as well as exercise one's own civil and socio-economic rights. Social and cultural divisions based on gender, race, religion, ethnicity, and language further increase such disparities. I feel less safe than any man to travel alone within and outside Nepal. I get better treatment in government offices, airports, restaurants, public transport if I speak English—and more so if in a particular accent! My clothes,

---

[1] Ramesh Kumar, "Nepal's Great Income Divide," *Nepali Times*, February 22, 2019, https://www.nepalitimes.com/banner/nepals-great-income-divide/ (accessed January 3, 2022); Amnesty International Nepal, CSRC-Nepal, and JuRI-Nepal, *Nepal: Land for Landless Peasants* (Kathmandu: AI Nepal, CSRC, JuRI Nepal, 2019), 6, https://www.amnesty.org/download/Documents/ASA3112212019ENGLISH.pdf (accessed January 3, 2022).

[2] The Minimum Hourly Wage for a Worker in Nepal is 0.66$, While Luxembourg has the Highest Minimum Wage in the World of 13.78$ per hour (all in USD). Himalayan News Service, "Minimum Monthly Wage of Workers Raised 11% to Rs 15,000" *The Himalayan Times*, May 4, 2021, https://thehimalayantimes.com/business/minimum-montly-wage-of-workers-raised-11-per-cent-to-rs-15000 (accessed January 3, 2022); "Minimum Wage by Country 2021," World Population Review, https://worldpopulationreview.com/country-rankings/minimum-wage-by-country (accessed January 3, 2022).

my body build, the food I eat, how I eat it, how I smell, the idea of clean-
liness, the music I listen to, the sports I play, etc., are weighed under
global cultural norms where some are considered more acceptable and
civilized than others.

Natural disasters shake up millions of lives world over, but they
affect the most vulnerable populations more. For instance, the processes
of recovering and rebuilding after the massive 2015 Nepal earthquake
have been disproportionately more challenging for women, Dalit, and
ethnically marginalized communities. More recently, rich countries have
received the far bulk of the world's COVID-19 vaccines, whereas the
rest of the world has received far less—yet another clear manifestation of
global inequality.

3   How Have the Places in Which You Have Lived and Worked Influenced Your View on Global Inequality?

My views on global inequality have profoundly been shaped by the places
I have lived in and traveled to. One of the first moments of realization
was as a little kid, when I was about 4 to 5 years old, and I could discern
the considerable differences in lifestyle of people in rural Nepal compared
to those of urban Kathmandu. I used to spend a month-long holiday with
my grandparents in our ancestral village in Gorkha every year. We had to
walk about four hours on foot from the bus stop to reach our village.
Basic necessities like water, food, sanitation, hospital, school, road, etc.,
were lacking or in very poor condition. I would see my father's school-
mates still ploughing their fields manually. The children I would play with
wore shabby clothes and looked malnourished. Generally, we would be
treated like some superior beings in the village.

My mother, also a social activist, used to regularly visit the slum area
at the Bishnumati riverbank. At times she would take me along and tell
me about the rescue of young girls living in those areas from human
trafficking. Those slums no longer exist today, but I still remember the
dilapidated semi-temporary structures, the lingering pungent smell, the
dingy, narrow alleys. It was my first look into the huge gap between the
living conditions of the urban poor and the average urban dwellers. In
1993, my mother got an opportunity to do her Master of Architecture at

Newcastle University, UK. She had to struggle with the Embassy authorities to take me along, whereas her male colleagues were readily allowed to take their family with them. In UK, I was racially bullied at school when I was 7 years old. But I particularly remember a Sudanese classmate being harassed more often. For me, what was striking about the UK was not just the easy availability but also the quality of food, education, housing, libraries, hard-surface roads, sports centers, and public transportation. By contrast, my maternal grandmother in Kathmandu had to wake up at odd hours in the night to collect tap water that was often unclean. And there in the UK, I saw clean twenty-four-hour running tap water, even hot if so desired! I realized how Nepal lacked even the most basic of amenities.

During the underground Maoist movement, while living incognito in different parts of India, I went to different schools and college, mostly government-run. When I got accepted to an elite college in Delhi (albeit itself a government-run one), all my classmates had been educated in private schools; I was the only one from a government school. (I obtained my higher secondary education (10 + 2) from NDMC Navyug School, Laxmibai Nagar, New Delhi, and I did my BA (Hons.) in Political Science from Lady Shri Ram College for Women, New Delhi from 2004–2007). In the college hostel, I remember having conversations about the condescending Delhiites and how others felt psychologically conscious and inferior to them. Some of us also conducted student trips to parts of India such as Orissa and Madhya Pradesh where Adivasis and farmers were fighting against corporate plunder and displacement. As an underground Maoist activist, I was more familiar with the unauthorized colonies and other areas inhabited by the urban poor, because that was where most of the migrant Nepali workers lived and some Nepali Maoists including my mother took shelter. (My mother was a Politburo member of the Communist Party of Nepal. Working in the party's headquarters team, the International Department and the Overseas Committee often required her to live incognito in different parts of India). It was utterly sad, infuriating and degrading to see most Nepali women and men doing menial jobs, working night shifts, and living precariously in a foreign land, and yet considering it a better alternative to remaining unemployed in one's own country.

4   WHAT ARE THE MAIN HISTORICAL CAUSES OF GLOBAL INEQUALITY?

I often wonder what makes inequality so all-pervasive. What is it about a country's system or societal structure that not only makes it possible for inequalities to endure for centuries, but also to reproduce inequalities in new forms? What is it about the global order that allows for inequality to persist worldwide, despite international organizations, global institutions, and leaders having repeatedly made commitments to its end? I have always heard that politics is about establishing equality and justice. And yet, every day is a different reality!

In agreement with the logic posed by studies on feudalism, colonialism, imperialism, capitalism, and neoliberal globalization, I believe that these have been central in creation and perpetuation of inequalities. At the heart of it all is consolidation of power and its sources. The concept of private property needs to be engaged with. Traditionally, property has been understood as land ownership although now we commonly use it in reference to other tangible as well as non-tangible assets. The act of possessing property creates a certain value that has material return (such as food, fuel, money, shelter, etc.) which also leads to non-material benefits such as societal status, the ability to be independent, leisure, etc. By making something inaccessible to all, it becomes more valuable for those who possess it. Historically, ownership, distribution, and concentration of property have occurred through conquest and violence. Property became a commodity, and integral to wealth generation. It has been a source of great power, not just economically but also politically and socio-culturally. This explains the logic of many forms of exploitation that perpetual inequalities. Why else would some countries colonize other countries? What else would explain the original relationship between landownership and voting rights? Why would the birth of a son be preferred over a daughter in certain communities, if not for property inheritance? What else would explain the corporate plunder of natural resources and displacement of indigenous communities? Why else would a majority of those who till the land not own that land? Why else would pharmaceutical companies so fiercely resist a temporary patent waiver for COVID-19 vaccines, even as thousands die every day? Additionally, through the mechanisms of state and international bodies that make laws and regulations with capitalist interests at center, inequality has acquired a structural and institutionalized form.

5   WHAT ARE THE MOST PRESSING CONTEMPORARY CHALLENGES CONCERNING GLOBAL INEQUALITY, AND HOW DO WE DEAL WITH THEM?

In my view, absolute poverty is the most pressing challenge. Although statistically, extreme poverty and hunger are said to have declined over the past few decades, there are still millions of people worldwide who continue to suffer without having access to basic amenities. Many live hand to mouth in the Global South. I know too many people who have worked hard throughout their life, but still cannot earn or save even a small fraction of what some people possess or inherit, without having to lift a finger. Poverty is not only a matter of numerical data and minimum income; it involves human lives and their rights and dignity as human beings. Other critical issues are gender and caste-based discriminations.

Global inequality is not an aberration or accidental occurrence, but a systematically structured phenomenon. The way forward is to make concerted organized efforts to end it. Within our individual countries, we need to push for more socio-economic rights to the poor and marginalized, fight corruption and bad governance, and make land reforms, tax reforms, etc. This itself is going to be a very tough fight, as it has been in Nepal. Therefore, we also need to look beyond the mere symptoms and manifestations of inequality, to tackle the larger structural and systemic crises that are global in nature. Hence, there is a need to form global solidarities and build global resistance.

Thinking Beyond Economics: The Politics of Inequalities

From Chile to New York City: Systemic Corruption and Oligarchic Domination

Camila Vergara

1 What Is Your Background and How Did You Become Interested in Global Inequality?

I am a political philosopher working on the intersection of inequality, corruption, and the law. My academic training has been a multidisciplinary effort to understand the basis of political authority and the principles of a democratic society, and how our political orders deviate from democratic principles, fueled by inequality and oligarchic domination. I grew up in Chile during the Pinochet dictatorship (1973–1990) and worked as a journalist writing on political economy during the country's transition to a limited democracy, in which a socially conservative, economically neoliberal worldview was constitutionally entrenched. As a journalist in the early 2000s, I covered stock markets and wrote investigative articles on the financial sector and the health care and pension systems. It was clear to me that the high degree of inequality in Chile was fueling a regime of accumulation at the very top, allowing for political corruption and the passing of laws favoring the powerful at the detriment

C. Vergara (✉)
University of Cambridge, Cambridge, UK
e-mail: cv370@cam.ac.uk

139
C. O. Christiansen et al. (eds.), *Talking About Global Inequality*,
https://doi.org/10.1007/978-3-031-08042-5_17

of the majority. Increasing inequality created an oligarchic political class that benefited from the status quo and therefore did nothing to decrease inequality or modify the patterns of accumulation that allowed the top 1% to appropriate more than one third of total wealth of the country.

Chile's oligarchic political structure, in which the wealthy and their corporations have a grip on the majority of the political class, is not an exception but increasingly the rule around the world. For almost a decade, I studied political and socioeconomic inequality in history and how hierarchical structures were put in place, not *despite* laws and institutions, but *through* them. I analyzed inequality and the constitutional orders it has generated in my book *Systemic Corruption. Constitutional Ideas for an Anti-Oligarchic Republic* (Princeton University Press, 2020). Therein, I theorize the global crisis of democracy from a structural point of view, arguing representative governments, as a regime type, suffer from a form of political decay linked to inequality and the oligarchization of society. A process by which the superrich control the political process, pushing for laws and policies that benefit big corporations at the detriment of common people. When the rules of the game consistently work for the powerful few and hurt the majority, then democracy has become oligarchic and in need of structural reform. This struggle to reign in the power of oligarchy cannot be done in one country alone; anti-oligarchic measures need to be adopted across nation-states as well as in international structures of governance.

2   WHAT IS GLOBAL INEQUALITY?

Global inequality is not a naturally occurring phenomenon but rather the result of unequal relations of power that are sustained and reproduced by a complex web of laws and regulations at the national, regional, and supranational levels, enforced or ignored depending on the actual power of political actors—the majority of them representing oligarchic interests. Moreover, global inequality is not the mere aggregation and quantification of similar degrees of inequality at the local, national, and regional levels, but rather the structural expression of different methods of oligarchic domination and the exploitation of human and natural resources around the world. Global inequality is only possible in an interconnected world in which the most powerful national oligarchs are able to expand their reach and exert domination at a global scale. Global inequality and social injustice advance together on the world stage. Conquest, colonialism, and hegemonic economic relations have allowed a few countries to become wealthy and powerful. These few wealthy and powerful countries are thus the main beneficiaries of a global economic growth in which poor countries bear the majority of the costs. From climate change to environmental pollution, global inequality, and the juridical and material structures that reproduce it, favor the already rich and powerful and burdens the most vulnerable within and among countries.

3   How Have the Places in Which You Have Lived and Worked Influenced Your View on Global Inequality?

I grew up partly on my grandfather's ranch in southern Chile. The son of a Spanish immigrant, he saved money and bought land in a remote place. He began to create a community around him, building houses for workers and their families. He was rich in property and took care of the people living on his land like family—not only paying health care and education bills, but with a deep concern for the wellbeing of those around him. It was during my first job as assistant *campera* (cowgirl) at the ranch at age 10 that I was confronted with the rigid socioeconomic hierarchy that separated me (granddaughter of the *patrón*) from the workers—despite us being equally high on our horses and equally buried, knee-deep in mud and cow muck. Listening to their conversations, I quickly realized that even if my grandfather was a "good boss," he was still a landlord who had the power to exploit, fire, and evict his workers if he so wanted to; that he chose not to, didn't change the relation of power in which he had a dominant position.

This capacity to identify unequal relations of power and their potential consequences in people's lives stayed with me, becoming essential to my work as a journalist. In my first job as a political economy reporter in 1999, through interviews with CEOs, ministers of finance and labor, ombudsman officers, and central bank economists, I learned much about the innerworkings of markets, the industries created around social services, and their interaction with laws and regulations at the national and international levels. I saw how sophisticated technical language and methods were deployed to rationalize both the disproportionate enrichment of the already wealthy and powerful, and the dispossession of the masses.

I was given a peek at how states defend oligarchic interests on the global stage when I briefly worked at the United Nations in New York as press attaché for Chile between 2009 and 2010. I witnessed with enormous frustration how non-binding or unenforceable resolutions declaring the socioeconomic rights of individuals were passed without much opposition—and with barely any impact on the ground—while motions undermining the economic interests of corporations based on wealthy countries didn't even make it to the floor for a general vote. I quickly realized that wealthy diplomats are part of the world's oligarchic political structure in which a few countries have veto power to deny the systemic change necessary to address global inequality. In my current position as a researcher and lecturer in topics of democracy and social justice, my goal has been to bring awareness of this inequality from an intersectional perspective—taking into account gender, ethnicity, class, and citizenship—so to make visible and accessible the diverse structural dominations that are enabled under the current world order.

4   WHAT ARE THE MAIN HISTORICAL CAUSES OF GLOBAL INEQUALITY?

The current patterns of accumulation and dispossession around the world originate at the foundation of the capitalist order: colonialism. The extraordinary amounts of natural resources extracted from the Americas, Africa, and Asia made possible accumulation of capital, the industrial revolution, and the rise of a new capitalist oligarchy that thrived in the nineteenth century's laissez-faire regimes in which there were few limits to labor exploitation and capital accumulation. By 1920, even if inequality had reached a level comparable to the degree of inequality present during feudal times, the devastation produced by the rise of fascism and the Second World War decreased inequality inside the US and Western Europe due to loss of accumulated wealth and post-war redistributive taxes—with top income tax rates of 70% or higher until

1980 in the US and above 60% in France until the late 1980s.[1] It is only after the neoliberal experiments in the 1970s and 1980s led by General Augusto Pinochet in Chile, Margaret Thatcher in the United Kingdom, and Ronald Reagan in the United States, that inequality begun to increase again.

In the 1980s, the neoliberal ideology of a lean state, in which taxes are low (current top income tax rate is 37% in the US and 40% in France), basic services are privatized, and regulations setting limits to the exploitation of labor and nature are scant and weak, swept the world. In the 1990s, international institutions played a crucial role in imposing more unequal patterns of accumulation within and between countries. The most consequential of such institutions was the IMF, which attached a laundry list of neoliberal requirements—the so-called Washington Consensus—to the loans given to developing countries.

In the US, which in the 1980s had already become the most powerful country in the world, inequality increased not only because of neoliberal reforms, but also because the US became the largest promoter of tax evasion, allowing for corporations to move to foreign jurisdictions to decrease their tax rates. Currently, about half of all the global profits that are shifted to tax havens are from US multinationals.[2] The massive amounts of wealth generated by rapid economic growth were poured into a deregulated financial system that ultimately enabled the 2008 crisis. Thanks to the massive transfer of wealth from the bottom to the top, due to neoliberal policies and cyclical crises, societies are today experiencing patterns of wealth accumulation comparable to those of the *ancien régime*, a period that ended with a popular revolution and the promise of a more equal world. We have reached a point in which global inequality has unveiled the domination of the superrich across borders, fueled by ever-increasing wealth stashed in tax havens, beyond the reach of state control(Fig. 1).

[1] See Thomas Piketty's long-term study of inequality in *Capital in the Twenty-First Century* (Cambridge: Cambridge University Press, 2014). For taxation see pp. 498–508.

[2] Kimberly A. Clausing, "Taxing Multinational Companies in the 21st Century" *The Brookings Institution*, January 28, 2020.

Fig. 1 "Organize your rage" spray-painted on a bus stop in downtown Santiago, Chile during the October 2019 popular uprising against the precarious living conditions imposed by the neoliberal model (Photograph taken by Camila Vergara)

5   WHAT ARE THE MOST PRESSING CONTEMPORARY CHALLENGES CONCERNING GLOBAL INEQUALITY, AND HOW DO WE DEAL WITH THEM?

Since global inequality is fueled by skewed patterns of accumulation at the national and international levels, the most pressing challenges relate to the ways in which our current juridical and regulatory structures are accelerating the rates of accumulation by the superrich. While tax havens allow for unlimited accumulation of wealth and undermine national efforts to tax local oligarchs, highly specialized lawyers dedicated to decrease companies' tax burden are constantly innovating and adapting legal codes to the interests of capital, setting precedents to rationalize and then

legalize unequal power relations.[3] The only way to revert the curre
patterns of accumulation and dispossession would be to eliminate the le
provisions that allow companies to be based in tax havens, and greatly
increase tax rates for billionaires.

Even if taxes on the wealthy forty years ago were double what they
are now, raising taxes today to those levels seems virtually impossible.
Representative governments have been coopted by special interests that
have pushed to eliminate regulations that limit the power of the wealthy,
and to pass laws benefiting the powerful at the detriment of the common
people and the environment. This process of oligarchization of power
through the existing institutions is what I have called *systemic corruption*, a form of political decay in which democratic forms enable a de
facto oligarchy that prevents any radical reform aimed at redistribution.
In order to properly deal with systemic corruption, countries need to
support anti-oligarchic laws aimed at curtailing the power of the wealthy.
However, given the oligarchic grip on politics, the probability of approval
and adequate enforcement of such laws is marginal. To properly deal with
global inequality, it is necessary then to radically reform the existing representative structures of power by establishing popular institutions able to
impose anti-oligarchic regulations and keep corruption in government in
check. It seems to me the most promising way to put global inequality
under control is by establishing local popular institutions, both in wealthy
and developing countries, able to reign in the power of oligarchs within
their respective national borders. Only the organized power of the many
has historically been a match for the power of the few. The efforts to
control global inequality should be placed not only on limiting the ability
of the wealthy to stash away their profits and avoid taxation, but also to
institutionally empower common people to control legislation and policy.

[3] See Katharina Pistor, *The Code of Capital: How the Law Creates Wealth and Inequality*,
(Princeton: Princeton University Press, 2019).

Making the Familiar Strange: Anthropological Reflections

Tania Murray Li

1 What Is Your Background and How Did You Become Interested in Global Inequality?

As a young child in the UK in the 1960s, I was steeped in class culture, trained implicitly to judge people by their accents. My father was in the British navy, his political horizon shaped by the Cold War and his belief in what he called "the free enterprise system". My mother was British, born and raised in Paraguay. Together they were eccentric, adventurous and socially progressive. They lost all their inherited family money in the early 1970s due to a failed business venture and my father was unemployed. I was saved by the welfare state—state education, state health care, money from unemployment insurance to buy groceries—so I did not have to leave school, go to work or marry young, the fate of many teenage girls when their families face hard times. My embodied cultural capital probably played a role too—an upper-class accent and *savoir faire* that mitigated my home-made clothing and lack of funds.

T. M. Li (✉)
University of Toronto, Toronto, ON, Canada
e-mail: tania.li@utoronto.ca

In 1975, my parents moved to Singapore and I finished high school exposed to modern Asian history and current affairs. War in Vietnam, the massacre of students in Thailand, Indonesia's invasion of East Timor and cultural revolution in China were the grist for my political awakening to questions of injustice, violence and state power. Travelling with school friends around Malaysia and Indonesia exposed me to different ways of living but global inequality did not strike me forcefully until 1977 when I spent a night in Mumbai due to a flight delay. Along the route to the hotel where the airline sent stranded passengers were huge drainpipes filled with families huddled around tiny lamps, their sleeping children sprawled on cardboard and covered with rags. I was 17 and the image stayed with me: this is not a normal way to live, I told myself, something happened to these people and I need to find out why they are living like this. Their experience became my enduring concern. I went on to study economic and political anthropology at Cambridge University and through decades of research on rural development I have continued to address the questions I posed then: how does inequality happen, and how does consigning people to live in drainpipes become normalized?

2   WHAT IS GLOBAL INEQUALITY?

Global inequality means that individuals have grotesquely different life chances based on the accident of their birth: their nationality, race, gender, class, health and the intersection of such elements. But what does this mean in human terms, and why is it so? To begin to address these questions, I propose a thought-experiment that borrows from my home discipline, anthropology, where we set out to make the strange familiar, and the familiar strange. So let's start with an observation that is familiar, even banal: a child of mine born in Canada has a vastly different life than a child born in a drainpipe on Mumbai's airport road. If we refuse to treat this observation as "just the way things are" and treat it instead as absolutely strange, then every process, practice and institutional arrangement that creates and sustains the unequal lives of these two children, and every ideology that seeks to justify it or cast it as natural or inevitable, must be called into question and subject to critical analysis.

Taking this approach to understanding what global inequality is, and how it works, opens up a rich field of empirical inquiry. In place of grand narratives, which suggest that all the people of the world are moving along a linear trajectory of progress such that they will—sooner or later—enjoy the life my child enjoys; or apocalyptic and fatalistic narratives that suggest whole segments of the global population are doomed to lead short and limited lives, a great many more specific questions need to be answered.[1] Within a rich country like Canada, what difference does race or gender make? Why are farmers in China so much better off than famers in India? Why is Malaysia so much further ahead on the UN's Human Development Index than its neighbour Indonesia (ranked 62 and 107 respectively, in 2020)?[2] How can we account for differences in life expectancy in different contexts, and so on. This type of inquiry requires attending to multiple spatial axes (not just north/south but rural/urban, national and sub-regional); and to the many social, cultural, political and institutional configurations that shape the life chances of a newborn child. All of these elements have histories: to ask why it is so is necessarily to ask how it came to be so, a question that can be addressed at many temporal and spatial scales. My point is that I cannot begin to make sense of what global inequality "is" without attending to specific constellations.

3   How Have the Places in Which You Have Lived and Worked Influenced Your View on Global Inequality?

Although based in Canada my main place of research for the past three decades has been Indonesia. Using ethnographic research methods that involve long stays and repeated visits to different rural places, I have tracked processes that produce inequality at close hand. In *Land's End,* I followed a group of indigenous highland farmers who took the step of privatizing their collective land and abandoning food production to focus on cacao, a global market crop that offered them a chance of prosperity. Class differentiation among farmers soon followed, as some did indeed prosper while others slid into destitution. For those who lost out the main vector was the small scale of their enterprises: they could not establish viable cacao farms nor could they revert to their former style of food production which required extensive land. They were forced to sell

---

[1] For some suggested lines of inquiry see James Ferguson and Tania Murray Li, *Beyond the "Proper Job:" Political-Economic Analysis After the Century of Labouring Man* (Cape Town: University of Western Cape, PLAAS Working Paper 51, 2018).

[2] http://hdr.undp.org/en/content/latest-human-development-index-ranking.

Fig. 1   Modest home of landless indigenous highlanders, standing among cacao trees owned by a neighbour in Indonesia (Photograph taken by Tania Murray Li)

land to cover survival costs, enabling some of their kin and neighbours to accumulate (Figs. 1 and 2).

Remarkably, my highland interlocutors had no critique of the inequality that emerged among them; they considered it a consequence of differences in luck and skill. But they could see that children born into newly-landless households would have radically diminished life chances. It was a situation for which they had no precedent: in the past hard-working highlanders could always clear a fresh patch of forest to restart their farms but now land was privately owned that pathway was closed.[3] Their critique was also blunted by the absence of a villain: farmers on a downward spiral had no one to blame. No agribusiness or government

---

[3] Tania Murray Li, *Land's End: Capitalist Relations on an Indigenous Frontier* (Durham, N.C.: Duke University Press, 2014).

Fig. 2 Home interior of landless indigenous highlanders (Photograph taken by Tania Murray Li)

programme had pushed them to privatize their land or try planting cacao; they were simply seeking a better life for their children, a legitimate aspiration. A different constellation of elements—more land or jobs, state subsidized credit to help them establish productive farms, state transfers or remittances to help farm families weather crises without taking on debt or selling land—would have produced different outcomes. In other agrarian contexts in Asia, Africa, Europe, the Americas, the constellation is indeed different, hence there is no single global story of inequality production.

In another research project (*Plantation Life*), I worked with an Indonesian colleague Pujo Semedi to track how inequality is produced through a very different set of processes—the arrival of massive state-backed plantations that grabbed land from villagers and left them without means of livelihood. This constellation also has a history—one that goes back to the colonial-era racism that remains embedded in Indonesia's land law, an authoritarian crony-corporate-military cabal installed in 1966 that is still in place, and a globally circulating discourse that equates corporate agriculture with productive efficiency, often without evidence.[4] "Global" elements (colonialism, global markets, racialized discourses about the inefficiency of small farms) have been present in rural Indonesia for 300 years but in this case too the forms of inequality they produce are situated and specific. In Thailand stronger land rights, more protective labour laws, and pro-farmer government policies have resulted in the virtual absence of corporate plantations.

4   WHAT ARE THE MAIN HISTORICAL CAUSES OF GLOBAL INEQUALITY?

Colonialism, capitalism, racism, misogyny, institutionalized oligarchy and their legitimating ideologies have been the main drivers of inequality, at least for the past five hundred years. These drivers emerged historically; they are not natural or inevitable. As economic historian Eli Cook argues in an incisive article, it is necessary to stress this point due to the current re-emergence of naturalizing explanations for inequality in at least four versions.[5] One version revives discredited variants on "mathematical law" that dictate a fixed ratio of inequality across time, or its exponential growth—a convenient explanation for inequality's current runaway acceleration. A second version cites what Cook calls "historical law"—how it was in the past is how it is and shall be. A third is "neoclassical law"— inequality as the result of difference in individual preferences, proclivities (to be frugal, enterprising, industrious) and productivity: in short, rich people are more productive and make good choices, from which their wealth "naturally" arises. The fourth is "genetic law", which attributes inequality to inborn qualities, often racialized.

As Cook points out, "laws" that have been thoroughly discredited in some quarters are periodically dusted off and given new life both in public discourse and in academia. Their revival in the context of the astronomical rise in global inequality over the past few decades is noteworthy; and it means that the work of critical scrutiny and fact-checking must be ramped up as well. Whatever their scientific garb or the language in which they are dressed—social Darwinism, efficiency, productivity—discourses that

---

[4] Tania Murray Li and Pujo Semedi, *Plantation Life: Corporate Occupation in Indonesia's Oil Palm Zone* (Durham, N.C.: Duke University Press, 2021).

[5] Eli Cook, "Naturalizing Inequality: The Problem of Economic Fatalism in the Age of Piketty", *Capitalism: A Journal of History and Economics* 1, no. 2 (2020): 338–378.

naturalize inequality must always be called into question. The alternative is to accept global inequality as inevitable, as if institutional arrangements, power and politics had nothing to do with it.

5   What Are the Most Pressing Contemporary Challenges Concerning Global Inequality, and How Do We Deal with Them?

The most pressing challenge I identify is shaped by my research focus on people—still half the world's population—who live in rural spaces and whose livelihoods depend on agriculture in whole or in part. Many of these people (not all) are on the brutal frontline of dispossession at the current time, whether through climate change, land seizure, crippling debt, abandonment by their governments or global trade arrangements that discount the value of their lives, labour and productive capacities. So there is an urgent need to stop dispossessory development in its tracks, before more damage is done and families are forced to live in drainpipes on the urban fringe. Preventing damage is slightly easier than restoration after the event, so it should take priority.

"Should" is a weak word. Indonesia is fantastically unequal. Oxfam reports that just four men own as much as one hundred million people.[6] The World Bank acknowledges that Indonesia has the third highest wealth concentration in the world after Russia and Thailand: 1% of the population own 50% of the wealth.[7] Yet the Bank's expert advice is to set this inconvenient problem aside and focus on skill development through education and foreign investment to create more formal sector jobs, that is, business as usual. The counterforce necessary to name the problem of inequality and tackle it head on is radically underdeveloped. In Indonesia and elsewhere, social movements that address inequality exist at multiple scales and work in diverse domains (land rights, poverty, climate change, gender). Too often, however, these movements are tamed by the forces

---

[6] Oxfam. *Towards a More Equal Indonesia*. 2017. https://www-cdn.oxfam.org/s3fs-public/bp-towards-more-equal-indonesia-230217-en_0.pdf.

[7] World Bank, *Indonesia's Rising Divide* (Jakarta and Washington: World Bank, 2016), 19.

of what Nancy Fraser calls "progressive neoliberalism".[8] This is a platform that concedes there is no alternative to the global apparatus that produces inequality and settles for small gains—women's shelters, sustainability certification or promises of corporate social responsibility and green investment. Polite dialogue among "stakeholders" and promises of technical fixes or win–win "solutions" enable global inequality to grow unchecked. They are another part of current common sense that must be called into question to secure space for the insurgencies to come.

---

[8] Nancy Fraser, "From Progressive Neoliberalism to Trump—and Beyond", *American Affairs* November 20 (2017).

From Buenos Aires to Belgrade

Agustín Cosovschi

1 WHAT IS YOUR BACKGROUND AND HOW DID YOU BECOME INTERESTED IN GLOBAL INEQUALITY?

I was born in Buenos Aires, Argentina in 1986. I grew up surrounded by an atmosphere of crisis, growing inequality, and a general feeling of disorientation and uncertainty. After a decade of financial crisis and hyper-inflation in the 1980s, Argentina entered a period of economic growth and modernization in the 1990s, but with widening social inequalities and increasing unemployment. In the early years of that decade, I saw my own father, a small industrialist working in the textile sector, go bankrupt. Many others around us had severe economic problems back then, and it was common to see members of the educated middle classes go through times of scarcity and precarization. At the same time, poverty became ever more visible and present, with beggars and rag-pickers becoming a normal part of everyday life in Buenos Aires.

A. Cosovschi (✉)
University Paris Nanterre, Paris, France
e-mail: agustin.cosovschi@efa.gr

French School in Athens, Athens, Greece

I became a teenager around the time of the Argentine social and economic meltdown in 2001, when the government of Fernando de la Rúa had to step down from power in the midst of deep financial crisis and massive protests by the middle classes and the urban and suburban poor. Immediately afterward, the country sank into sovereign default, and a sudden and violent devaluation of the peso was introduced, which also increased poverty further. All of this was in many ways the peak of the crisis of previous years. But still, the violence on the streets, the strong criticism of political parties and the rise of new social movements and new political leaders meant that most of us experienced those years as a turning point.

My teenage years were shaped by that experience and also by the actions of social and political movements that reacted to that crisis putting forward a new agenda of social inclusion. The beginning of Nestor Kirchner's government in 2003, all in a regional context characterized by the rise of progressive movements in Latin America (including the Partido dos Trabalhadores in Brazil, the Frente Amplio in Uruguay and the Movimiento al Socialismo in Bolivia), inspired me to take up studies in sociology and to simultaneously develop different forms of activism for some time. My studies in sociology allowed me to get acquainted with different theories that attempted to explain social and economic inequality on a local and global level, from classical Marxism to more recent dependency theory and critical perspectives on the global political economy. Moreover, even though my experience in activism barely lasted for about two years, it constituted an important part of my political education and allowed me to have experiences that otherwise would have been difficult to have, such as meeting activists from older generations and getting to know marginalized urban neighborhoods and slums from within, and studying militant Marxist thought in a way that has left imprints on my thinking until today.

Years later, my interest in Marxism and my own family background as an Eastern European Jew made me become more and more fascinated by the history of Eastern Europe. Some part of my family background had probably influenced my thinking in earlier years: my grandfather from my mother's side, as many other Argentine Jews, had been a committed communist, while my grandfather from my father's side, a Jew born in Romania and exiled in times of Nazism, was never even close to embracing left-wing ideas, but lived through extreme poverty as a child and always conveyed a strong respect for the poor and the workers.

These family connections notwithstanding, when I decided to pursue a Master's in History and then a Ph.D. in History focusing on Eastern Europe, it was socialist Yugoslavia that came to the center of my interests. On the one hand, because I did not want to engage directly with the cultures, languages and places that had been at the center of my family's history. On the other hand, because the very particular geopolitical position of Yugoslavia, halfway between the East and the West, reminded me somehow of the geopolitical position of Argentina. That impression was even reinforced when I started traveling to Serbia and Croatia, and started meeting people who, probably because of a certain "Southern charm," but also because of their cynicism and fatalism, reminded me constantly of the Argentines (and still do). Last but not least, Yugoslav policy vis-à-vis the Third World, its commitment to non-alignment and Belgrade's official policy of seeking a path to socialism away from Soviet guidelines also had a strong echo with my own experience as a Latin American.

2   What Is Global Inequality?

I see global inequality as a structural feature of the capitalist system: a persistent trend throughout modernity often expressed through colonial or neocolonial relations, but which has taken new and different forms since the rise of globalization since the 1970s. Some forms of global inequality have tended to diminish in the last few decades: as globalization has allowed for the inclusion of certain countries and regions in larger global value chains, many nations have had the opportunity to profit from capitalist expansion and uplift millions of people from poverty, especially in Asia. On the contrary, other forms of inequality have tended to expand, such as regional imbalances within national economies, because certain geographical areas and economic sectors inside the countries themselves manage to enter well and efficiently into the economy of globalization, while others find themselves excluded and replaced through offshoring and by the inclusion of new technology.

In the era of globalization, I reckon, the weakening of the role of the state has proved to be fatal, especially in Western societies: the state has often gone from being a central agent in economic development to a mere facilitator of globalization processes, and its capacities in social intervention have also been reduced, with state agencies no longer being able to

guarantee social inclusion, but barely compensating through social benefits for the exclusionary effects of offshoring. Thus, I see global inequality
as a problem that not only concerns the "global South" anymore. New
global forms of exclusion have created armies of marginalized in several
wealthy economies, as in the case of the Rust Belt in the United States or
the weakened industrial north in France, and threaten to destabilize our
societies more and more.

3   How Have the Places in Which You Have Lived and Worked Influenced Your View on Global Inequality?

I have spent most of my life in Buenos Aires. But for some years now,
I have been based in Paris. Living in France, a country where globalization has hit the industrial sector and traditional workers very hard,
where unemployment has been a structural feature for decades and where
disbalances between the city and the countryside are often shocking,
has also allowed me to become aware of the negative consequences of
globalization in what we usually consider to be "the developed world."
Paris combines obscene levels of wealth with crude levels of poverty and
marginality, where young and rich executives drink and eat out often
without even noticing the growing army of beggars that walk right next
to them. All of this has made me increasingly aware of the dysfunctional-
ities of the current system. This vision of a "First World" full of patches
of "Third World" inequality has made me more sensitive to the need to
rethink inequality as a global phenomenon and not predominantly as a
problem concerning the countries of the Global South, as it used to be
during much of the twentieth century.

4   What Are the Main Historical Causes of Global Inequality?

I believe that the main historical causes of global inequality lay in different
and diverging histories of national development, but also in the consequences of colonialism, in the persistence of neocolonial relations and in
the reaffirming of imbalances that tend to be reproduced and often aggravated by the unequal terms of global exchange. There have been notable
cases of economic and social development in peripheral countries through

very effective modernization strategies, often coupled with authoritarian politics, such as in the case of China and Vietnam. Certainly, globalization has allowed several economies in Asia, Africa and Latin America to uplift millions of people from extreme poverty. But the distribution of wealth inside national economies has tended to be unequal, and the dynamics of the global economy have tended to fragment national economies all around the globe by creating "niches of globalization" that coexist with post-industrial niches of poverty and marginality. Hence, I believe that we must strive to find better and more efficient strategies of inclusion: not to roll back globalization, but to correct its imbalances. I reckon that analyzing the history of economic thought and alternative projects of development can be illuminating in that regard and can help us think critically about current developments.

5   What Are the Most Pressing Contemporary Challenges Concerning Global Inequality, and How Do We Deal with Them?

I see at last two great challenges ahead. The first one is related to the survival of democracy: many cases of successful modernization in peripheral countries have relied on strong authoritarian regimes which curbed political freedoms in order to control the destabilizing effects of economic and social modernization. China is perhaps the clearest example, but a similar argument can be made about other countries during the twentieth century; Brazil in the 1960s and 1970s, South Korea and many others. Those examples of successful economic development mixed with authoritarianism, along with current trends in Western countries, which support the idea of taming globalization through strong political rule and nationalism, can eventually contribute to spreading the idea that limiting democracy is a condition for successful economic development. That, I believe, would be a very unfortunate lesson to make.

The second challenge is related to the environmental limits of current models of development, which will certainly become obvious in years to come. I believe that this ultimately demands radical strategies and initiatives in terms of changing the modes of production and consumption following more rational and ecological criteria. However, rethinking these modes of production and consumption means reassessing globalization as it currently stands. The leaders of the main economic powers of the world do not seem to be ready or willing to engage in such initiatives beyond minor changes, and perhaps more importantly, transnational capital will not accept giving up a share of its gains for environmental reasons. Given the endless list of leaders who have failed in their confrontation with transnational capital during the last few decades, from Mitterrand in France to Tsipras in Greece, optimism is hard to justify. I still believe that the solution must come from politics, but the sheer lack of efficient reformist political forces in the most influential countries of the world paints a very grim picture in that regard.

Perspectives from the South: An Islander Woman Speaks

Sheila Bunwaree

1 What Is Your Background and How Did You Become Interested in Global Inequality?

My great-grandparents came to Mauritius from India as indentured laborers to work in the sugarcane fields, after the abolition of slavery in 1835. Being a fourth-generation woman of Indian-indentured-laborer-descent, I have, while growing up, often had the opportunity of listening to narratives around issues of exclusion, discrimination and injustices recounted by both my maternal and paternal grandmothers. Stories of hardships and the dehumanizing experiences recounted also included those of families of slave descent. The very beginnings of Mauritius, where I was born, point to a history of exploitation, oppression, and unequal relations.

Having chosen history and geography as disciplines, among a host of others, during my secondary schooling in the early 70s, provided me with some hope of further understanding my history and creole identity as an islander woman. However, this quickly turned into disillusion.

S. Bunwaree (✉)
University of Mauritius, Moka, Mauritius
e-mail: Sheila_bun@yahoo.co.uk

I expected these two school subjects would help me anchor my grand-mothers' narratives and better understand how the oppressed, contesting the different forms of inequality and prejudices they faced, developed a sense of 'agency' and resilience. But nothing of the sort happened. Instead, I had to study European Medieval history and the geography of faraway places.

This made me question inequalities and hierarchies in knowledge production and distribution, contributing to my understanding of global inequality. The imposition of certain disciplines and the necessity of deconstructing colonial knowledge systems haunted me for a long time, influencing my choice of field of study at university. I read sociology and economics (a joint honors degree course) at Swansea University from 1977–1980. The course was an eye-opener, permitting me to theorize my grandmothers' narratives, built on the intersectionalities of race/ethnicity, gender, and class. These new interpretations triggered more questions and further developed my interest in global inequality.

This interest was honed by the Master's course in Development Studies that I undertook as a young graduate at the Center for Development Studies, at Swansea itself from 1980–1981. The course was generally reserved for mid-career development practitioners from the developing world. Every single module of the M.Sc. program gravitated around issues of inequality, exclusion, and poverty. One development practitioner from the copper belt of Zambia, for instance, presented a case study of how Zambia's mining industry declined, contributing to the country's economic downfall and indebtedness. This was prior to the country's adoption of the structural adjustment programs. How the latter then contributed to the further impoverishment of the country and other places on the African continent was better understood, providing me with greater insights on world politics and development.

With hindsight, my interest in global inequality goes as far back as my childhood days. Every school holiday, I accompanied my dad, a commu-nity development officer cum social worker, to the villages and deprived zones of Mauritius. Foreign and local experts were invited to give semi-nars on different aspects of development, inequality, and poverty so as to find ways of solving problems at the grassroots level. The articulation between the local and the global, although not spelt out, could be sensed.

2   WHAT IS GLOBAL INEQUALITY?

Global inequality is a reflection of differentiated patterns of production, deep-rooted power rivalries, shifting geo-strategic relations. Geographical boundaries, the North–South divide and how countries belonging to these two blocks, further classified as high-income, middle-income, upper middle-income and low-income countries, assist us in appreciating the significance of unequal levels of development. Such divides also make one more cognizant of how the most powerful pull the levers to their own advantage, reproducing the same old forms of inequality.

Global inequality is also about how globalization creates winners and losers. Catching up with the big players, trying to grow and deliver development to their people; less developed countries are confronted with an interplay of external and internal dynamics making it hard to close the gaps between the wealthy and the poor, across and within nations.

Sometimes, the absence of ethical and humane governance within frameworks of poor leadership translates into political elites colluding with superpowers, often provoking conflicts, bad governance, and corruption. The latter has become a disease of many political and economic systems, siphoning off the much-needed resources to attain the United Nations Sustainable Development Goals (Agenda 2030) as well as the African Union Agenda 2063. When development is persistently gnawed at, global inequality is on the rise.

Global inequality can also be seen through climate change lenses. Mauritius is a negligible emitter of carbon gas emissions, but an important victim of global warming. The contradictions of development sometimes make small island states, such as my own, become a 'victim' of its own success and not necessarily at par with others, when it comes to climate finance. The complex interplay of history, politics, economic, and climate diplomacy can also be important drivers of global inequality. This is an area which demands further investigation.

The international division of labor within the dominant neoliberal order and the plight of migrant workers laid bare by the COVID-19 pandemic also speak volumes about global inequality, pushing some of us to advocate for alternative development paradigms. The current economic order is one void of a common humanity. In short, global inequality is about unequal distribution of resources, the trampling of fundamental human rights and the suppressing of people's life chances. Assetlessness, voicelessness, and powerlessness remain some of its principal characteristics.

3   HOW HAVE THE PLACES IN WHICH YOU HAVE LIVED AND WORKED INFLUENCED YOUR VIEW ON GLOBAL INEQUALITY?

My first personal experience with global inequality was when I visited India for the first time some 40 years ago. I was treated to a holiday by my parents after successfully completing my university studies. As I stepped out from the luxurious Mumbai hotel, some 50 meters down the road, I saw a string of shacks standing in deep contrast to the beautifully manicured gardens of the hotel. People were literally bathing on the streets, children eating in the most unhygienic conditions, while one woman was screaming in labor pain as she was about to give birth on the very pavement where their flimsy homes were erected. These images of the horror of poverty and inequality are etched in my memory. I revisited India some 15 years later, on a collaborative research project with colleagues at the TATA Institute of Social Sciences in Mumbai. The shacks were no longer there, the roads next to the hotel were cleaner, but this did not mean that poverty and inequality had disappeared. I was told that the shacks were destroyed by the government. The people were displaced, and some relocated to the backstreets of the hotel in an attempt to hide the ugly face of poverty from tourists.

Inequality is neither a natural nor an inevitable state of affairs. It is often the result of policies, laws, institutions, socio-cultural norms, and practices, governance deficits and the unequal distribution of wealth and power. The latter was made more visible to me during my Ph.D. years in Melbourne, from 1989–1992, where I was on a generous commonwealth scholarship. Seeing other students, particularly from the developing world, toiling very long hours at work to meet the cost of their studies and make ends meet, triggered many questions in me. I also had the opportunity to meet a few Mauritian families who had migrated to Australia in the late 1960s and early 1970s around Mauritius' independence in 1968. Some of these families' stories revolved around the deep structures of poverty and legacies of discrimination which they had to endure for many years. Others saw the migration wave as a result of the fear of the Hindu hegemony in Mauritius at the time. The complex interplay of class, race/ethnicity and gender was once more made evident in the context of the great Mauritian migration story of the early 1970s. Their testimonies also helped me to gauge how people's life chances are shaped by different opportunities and how contemporary forms of migration lie at the heart of global inequality.

In 2000, I was selected for the post of Director of Research at the Council of Social Sciences in Africa (CODESRIA) in Dakar, Senegal. The job gave me the opportunity to travel all over Africa, meet researchers, policymakers, and diplomats, participate in a large number of conferences, workshops, and policy dialogues on different facets of development. All the scholarly work I read as a young adult such as Walter Rodney's *How Europe Underdeveloped Africa*, Albert Memmi's *The Colonizer and the Colonized*, Frantz Fanon's *The Wretched of the Earth*, to name a few, resonated with me from different perspectives, while based on the continent. The paradox of Africa—'so rich and yet so poor'—took a new significance.

My stint as Senior Researcher at the Center for Conflict Resolution in Cape Town, South Africa from 2009–2011, and the very many academic meetings we organized on themes related to conflict, development and gender, made the various ramifications of global inequality on African women's lives clearer. Fresh perspectives on how the global financial crisis impacted on the daily existential conditions of women were obtained. More than ever before, finding African solutions to African problems has become most urgent especially if global inequality is to be addressed in a significant manner. I also had the direct responsibility of organizing gender training sessions, with women in conflict zones. This opened up the debates and engagement for a deeper interrogation of global inequality from an African feminist perspective. Having more women's voices at the decision-making table cannot be emphasized enough. Addressing global inequality also meant applying gender lenses to the complex interplay of factors, within the rapidly changing multilateral set up, so as to assist in transforming the world to make it a better, more inclusive and more just place for all.

Prior to Cape Town, I spent a few months, as a guest researcher, at the Nordiska Africa Institute in Uppsala, Sweden, researching on 'Governance and Gender' in Africa, with a special focus on Mauritius. That debates on governance and gender would be incomplete without factoring in discussions on human rights and capabilities became more obvious to me. The significance of these on the evolving nature of global inequality also became more apparent.

4   WHAT ARE THE MAIN HISTORICAL
CAUSES OF GLOBAL INEQUALITY?

Global inequality can be attributed to imperialism and colonialism, persistent unequal trading arrangements, structural adjustment programs and the related debt trap, the technological divide as well as patriarchy. These factors are often interspersed with other ground realities—political, social, economic, and cultural—thus further shaping inequality across and within countries.

Imperialism can be seen as the root cause of contemporary forms of inequality. Closing the inequality gaps across and within nations remains a problem, exacerbated by the deleterious impacts of the COVID-19 pandemic and the new configuration of globalization. Decolonization, albeit good for ending certain forms of oppression and inequality, did not necessarily get instrumentalized to change the unequal economic world order and to ensure that there is no succumbing to new forms of colonialism.

Expectations that newly 'decolonized' countries, in the 1960s would be able to engage world trade on more equal terms simply did not materialize. Unequal trading arrangements and rules favoring the rich and powerful persisted. This meant the continuation of old inequality gaps. Whether the WTO has been able to assist in tackling global inequality remains a question only partially answered.

The IMF structural adjustment programs, and the conditionalities that many developing countries were subjected to, meant greater poverty and inequality. Different types of IMF mandated policy conditions such as fiscal policy reforms, curtailing government expenditure on sectors like education and health, have retarded development. Trapped in debt spirals, some countries became increasingly dependent on their former Western colonial masters and/or fell prey to emerging powers/new players such as China and India. These two nations have entered into a new 'scramble' for resources to meet their insatiable wants, rendering global inequality more complex than ever before.

While technology is often seen as a source of progress, as having a capacity to help lower market barriers and costs, opening up a range of opportunities, its potential to deepen inequality must not be underestimated. Modern technology can easily displace unskilled workers, creating huge levels of unemployment and associated societal ills. Artificial intelligence and robotization is leading to severe loss of jobs, creating ghost towns in certain spaces, and leading to new forms of inequality. Economies with sophisticated technologies, high innovation capacity and skilled human capital can easily turn digital and become more productive, causing other kinds of inequality gaps between countries.

Another element of the international division of labor is the care economy. The COVID-19 pandemic has shone a light on diverse forms of inequality, including those of the care economy. The latter consists of looking after the elderly, the sick, the vulnerable, the disabled and children both within the paid and unpaid spheres. Women remain disproportionately represented in this sector and are important contributors to making the wheels of the world system turn. Patriarchy remains embedded within the internationalist capitalist system and constitutes a major cause of global inequality.

5   What Are the Most Pressing Contemporary Challenges Concerning Global Inequality, and How Do We Deal with Them?

The debates on the challenges of reconciling 'lives and livelihoods,' vaccine inequity, disruption in food supply chains, the poor facing diverse kinds of risks and vulnerabilities, the SDGs (particularly SDG 5 on gender equality, taking a severe blow in the context of the COVID-19 pandemic) as well as the Anthropocene age, that we have entered, require us to revisit mainstream economic thought and its obsession with growth. Orthodox economics, which continues to see GDP per head as a measure of welfare, and the ecological footprint of those who are solely guided by the maximization of profits, remain major challenges we are confronted with, in these pandemic times. Another major challenge is the absence of strong commitment to climate and gender justice and the inability to adopt an alternative development model, whose underpinnings are inclusion, fairness, and equity. In short, sustainability should be at the core of the new paradigm and the playing field across and within nations should be leveled.

Ethical and humane governance are required both at the international and national level. Institutions of higher learning across borders should play a critical role in building a pool of people with a strong global social conscience. Transnational alliances between civil society groups should be strengthened so that the slide toward authoritarianism and growing inequality is halted. More efforts should be put in at all levels to close gender gaps and bring more women into positions of decision-making—not only for a politics of numbers and representation, but for a politics of ideas and transformation, so that the alternative development paradigm proposed can be urgently brought about.

INDEX

Printed by Printforce, United Kingdom

SIXTY
IS THE
NEW
ASSASSIN

A NOVEL
BY SHESH

Published by Westland Books, a division of Nasadiya Technologies Private Limited, in 2024

No. 269/2B, First Floor, 'Irai Arul', Vimalraj Street, Nethaji Nagar, Alapakkam Main Road, Maduravoyal, Chennai 600095

Westland and the Westland logo are the trademarks of Nasadiya Technologies Private Limited, or its affiliates.

ISBN: 9789360457778

10 9 8 7 6 5 4 3 2 1

This is a work of fiction. Names, characters, organisations, places, events and incidents are either products of the author's imagination or used fictitiously.

Typeset by Jojy Philip

Printed at Nutech Print Services, India

This book is dedicated to Radhika,
my reason for living.

And killing.